AMERICA'S CUP 1851 TO 1992

The Official Record of America's Cup XXVIII & the Louis Vuitton Cup

AMERICA'S CUP
1851 TO 1992

*The Official Record of America's Cup XXVIII
& the Louis Vuitton Cup*

PHOTOGRAPHERS

Carlo Borlenghi

Bob Grieser

Sally Samins

Kirk Schlea

Deann J. Shier

Kaoru Soehata

AUTHOR

Michael Levitt

ART DIRECTOR

Craig Fuller

EDITOR-IN-CHIEF

Christopher G. Capen

GRAPHIC ARTS CENTER PUBLISHING · PORTLAND OREGON

SUPPORT PROVIDED BY YACHTING MAGAZINE, EASTMAN KODAK AND CHEVROLET MOTOR DIVISION

*AMERICA'S CUP 1851 TO 1992: THE OFFICIAL RECORD OF AMERICA'S CUP XXVIII & THE
LOUIS VUITTON CUP* IS PUBLISHED UNDER AN EXCLUSIVE LICENSING AGREEMENT WITH
THE 1992 AMERICA'S CUP ORGANIZING COMMITTEE, AMERICA'S CUP PROPERTIES, INC.
AND THE SAN DIEGO YACHT CLUB.

THIS BOOK WAS PRODUCED BY PUBLISH '92, L.P. (SAN DIEGO, CA) AND INTERNATIONAL
MANAGEMENT GROUP (IMG) PUBLISHING (NEW YORK, NY). MARKETING AND
PRODUCTION MANAGEMENT WAS PROVIDED BY
ARLEN PUBLISHING (SAN DIEGO) AND IMG PUBLISHING (NEW YORK).
1420 KETTNER BLVD., SUITE 300 • SAN DIEGO, CALIFORNIA 92101 • 619/525-7000
22 EAST 71ST STREET • NEW YORK, NY 10021 • 212/772-8900
PRESIDENT, ARLEN PUBLISHING • DOUGLAS A. AUGUSTINE
VICE PRESIDENT, IMG PUBLISHING • ARTHUR KLEBANOFF
PROJECT DIRECTOR • CHRISTOPHER G. CAPEN
ASSISTANT PROJECT DIRECTOR • J. CHRISTOPHER ROSS
ART DIRECTOR • CRAIG FULLER
COPY EDITOR • DOUGLAS LOGAN
PRODUCTION MANAGER • HELEN CORONADO
ASSISTANT SALES MANAGER • CHRISTIAN SCHNABEL

ISBN 1-55868-105-1 (ENGLISH LANGUAGE EDITION)
LIBRARY OF CONGRESS CATALOG NUMBER 92-70540

ENGLISH EDITION PUBLISHED BY GRAPHIC ARTS CENTER PUBLISHING COMPANY
P.O. BOX 10306 • PORTLAND, OREGON 97210 • 503/226-2402
PRESIDENT • CHARLES M. HOPKINS
EDITOR-IN-CHIEF • DOUGLAS A. PFEIFFER

DISTRIBUTED IN NORTH AMERICA AND ENGLAND BY GRAPHIC ARTS CENTER.
DISTRIBUTED IN ITALY BY GRUPPO UGO MURSIA EDITORE S.P.A..
DISTRIBUTED IN AUSTRALIA BY DARLING HARBOUR YACHT CLUB.

PUBLISHED IN FRENCH BY EDITION OUEST FRANCE, PARIS.
PUBLISHED IN GERMAN BY EDITION MARITIM, HAMBURG.
PUBLISHED IN ITALIAN BY SPERLING & KUPFER, MILAN.
PUBLISHED IN JAPANESE BY SHOGAKUKAN PUBLISHING, TOKYO.
PUBLISHED IN SPANISH BY EDICIONES FOLIO, BARCELONA.

LIMITED EDITION PUBLISHED BY MYSTIC SEAPORT MUSEUM STORES (MSMS),
MYSTIC, CONN. AND PRODUCED BY LONGSTREET PRESS, MURIETTA, GEORGIA.
PRESIDENT, MSMS • THOMAS A. AAGESEN
SALES DIRECTOR, MSMS • DOROTHY A. HAZLIN
DIRECTOR, SPECIAL PROJECTS, LONGSTREET PRESS • WALT FULLER

ROYAL EDITION DISTRIBUTED BY:
SQUARE TRUST CO., LTD., TOKYO, JAPAN
3T & ASSOCIATES, INC., GLENDALE, CA U.S.A.

PRINTED AND BOUND IN JAPAN BY DAI NIPPON PRINTING COMPANY, LTD.
ASSISTANT GENERAL MANAGER • KOHEI HIRANO
SALES REPRESENTATIVE, TOKYO • SHUICHI SEINO
SALES MANAGER, LOS ANGELES • KOHEI TSUMORI

CONTENTS

A New Tack for a New Era

By Walter Cronkite

IT WOULD BE DIFFICULT to exaggerate the influence of the America's Cup competition on the sport of sailing. Every few years, sailors of all descriptions, from the most convivial yacht club racer to the self-sufficient cruising singlehander direct their attention to the Cup. There are several reasons, aside from the excitement of the racing itself, for this almost universal focus.

All sailors respect the skills it takes to move a vessel through wind and waves at top speed, and the Cup competition is a gathering place for many of the most skillful — Olympians, national and world champions, ocean-racers and dinghy specialists, match-racing experts, navigators and tacticians. Supporting the sailors on the water are scores of designers, boatbuilders, riggers, sailmakers, hardware engineers and, now, computer specialists. These legions are drawn to the America's Cup because, for 141 years, it has been the jewel in sailing's crown.

At this level of competition there are no lapses in concentration and very few mistakes. Through an ever-shifting interplay of fluid elements — air and water — the boats are sailed with the utmost mastery and precision. When a flaw emerges, in tactics, in sailhandling, or in any number of other crucial areas, a race is often lost. Yet, no matter which boat is ultimately successful, it is as thrilling for a sailor to see this concert of skills as it is for a musician to bear witness to a brilliant symphony.

We watch because we know that many of the advances in hull and rig design, sailmaking, instrumentation, and sailing technique that are evident on the Cup course today may well be parts of our own sailing lives in the coming months and years. And we are drawn to the event because the whole dazzling coalescence of talent and technology is so often brought about by intriguing personalities, some eccentric, some charismatic, some comic, some tragic, all hard-driven in their quest to defend the Auld Mug — or to make off with it. Their names are the colorful threads in the fabric of America's Cup history — Dunraven, Lipton, Sopwith, and Vanderbilt; and in more recent years Bich, Turner, Bond, Fay, Conner, and Koch.

If there is another sport that brings about such an intense concentration of skilled competitors, scientific knowledge, and mechanical ingenuity, it might be auto racing — although most drivers, one might suppose, would be hard put to contend with undulating racetracks and horsepower dependent entirely upon the momentary whims of nature.

It has not always been easy to follow the intricate path of the America's Cup in the last decade. In 1983, after 132 years undisturbed, the Cup was wrested from Dennis Conner and the New York Yacht Club by the wing-keeled *Australia II* and moved half a world away. In 1987 Conner retrieved it and brought it to San Diego. Then came the audacious challenge from New Zealander Michael Fay. There were court battles, a bizarre and uneven match between two miracles of modern engineering — Fay's 130-foot sloop and Conner's much faster (naturally!) catamaran — then more court battles. By the time the judges decided that the Cup would remain in San Diego, even the most devoted America's Cup observers were beginning to fear that the oldest continuous competition in sports might have been fatally besmirched.

If the lopsided match between the enormous sloop and the wing-masted catamaran proved anything, it was that the 12-Meter had sailed well past its useful era. It was clear to virtually everyone involved in the America's Cup that in the future the event would have to incorporate the technological advances that already were parts of top-level racing.

Even as the competition seemed to be dissolving in the acrimony of the courtroom, it was being overhauled behind the scenes by a consortium of top yacht designers and organizers. There were several thoughtful and remarkably cooperative meetings between designers, builders, and the stewards of the Cup in the fall of 1988. From those meetings emerged the new International America's Cup Class yacht — 75 feet long, much lighter than a 12-Meter, and with much greater sail area. These boats are powerful, graceful, fast, and difficult to sail. They have been given a new America's Cup course, including three reaching legs in which they can fly huge asymmetrical spinnakers, and reach speeds of 16 knots. There is a saying that watching yacht racing is as exciting as watching the grass grow. If it was ever true, it is true no longer.

Confirmation that the designers' and organizers' ideas had been on target arrived in San Diego with a flock of eight challenging syndicates from seven nations, and two defense syndicates. In all, 28 of the new America's Cup boats were built for the 1992 event — an astounding concentration of money and effort, but perhaps less astounding when one considers that the Cup is more than a yacht-racing trophy. It is also a kind of measuring cup, seen by many as a gauge not only of a nation's sailing prowess, but of its technical capabilities, and its willingness to compete in a vastly complex melding of science and sport at an international level.

Two challenging groups, from the new, freestanding political entities of Russia and Croatia did not make it to the starting line. It would be fair to assume that their absence was due to a basic ordering of priorities, but when one hears reports that the latter group worked feverishly to complete construction of its boat as bullets flew nearby, one begins to recognize the importance that can be attached to this event.

While there was no doubt that the revamped competition had sparked the interest of nations around the world, there were also indications of sailing's ability to bridge political and cultural boundaries: New Zealander Chris Dickson steered the Japanese boat, while Americans Rod Davis and Paul Cayard served as helmsmen aboard the challengers from New Zealand and Italy. German Ralf Steitz worked as pitman aboard Dennis Conner's boat. This internationalism was, in fact, commonplace throughout the fleet. It was a far cry from the competitions of even a few years ago, but when barriers are falling everywhere, the world of the America's Cup could hardly be expected to exempt itself. Sailors have always been good travelers and adaptable companions.

This book is the official chronicle of the first event in the newest epoch of America's Cup history. It will be a valuable reference for all sailors who welcome, as I do, the new boats, the new course, and the new spirit behind this greatest of sailing challenges.

CHAPTER ONE

FROM 1851 TO 1990

An America's Cup History

On August 22, 1851, America won a race around the Isle of Wight for the Hundred Guinea Cup. The America's Cup came to be named after her.

O N MAY 1, 1851, A NEW YORK newspaper reported that "Mr. W. H. Brown, foot of Twelfth Street, has finished his yacht for the World's Fair, and will test on Friday her powers of sailing in a match with Mr. Stevens's yacht *Maria.*" *America*, the boat Mr. Brown built, would in time set in motion and lend her name to the international sailing competition that became known as the America's Cup. One hundred and forty-one years later, the oldest trophy in sports in continuous competition remains an ultimate symbol of excellence and national achievement. The competition has survived because the America's Cup combines physical skill, courage, technology, execution, and intelligence unlike any other sport.

If the America's Cup is the most venerable trophy in sports, it is also the most contentiously fought-over. The reasons for this have to do not only with the desirability of the prize, but with the changing nature of the rules and their episodic enforcement; with the fact that the keeper of the Cup plays a large part in

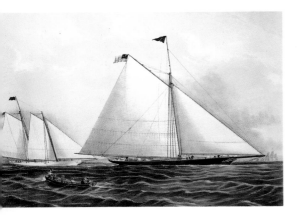

Maria *was also owned by the family of John Cox Stevens, who headed the* America *syndicate.* Maria *was designed by Robert Stevens, the brother of John Cox. If* America *had been faster "than any vessel in the United States brought to compete with her," the syndicate would have paid $30,000 for her.* Maria, *however, beat* America, *and the syndicate paid $20,000 for her.* America, *then painted white, is the second boat in this painting.*

One of the earliest photographs of America, *taken in 1852 or 1853. Distinguishing features were her very fine bow, low freeboard, well-raked masts, and simple sailplan — specifically a lack of topsails. The topsails in this photograph, however, show she was rerigged. After the 1851 race,* America *was sold at a $5000 profit to John de Blaquiere, an Englishman, and rerigged for cruising.*

making and enforcing the rules; and, of course, with the personalities of those who defend it or pursue it.

A large part of America's Cup competition has always involved the sheer willingness to stand firm and wage war. The kind of person who goes "softly into the night," as that expression has it, doesn't do well in the America's Cup. Indeed it can be argued that contentiousness is one of the things that has helped keep the America's Cup competition vital.

To understand what the America's Cup is, it is helpful to focus on some of the more important matches to know what it has been.

AMERICA: 1851

On that same May Day in 1851, the International Exhibition, or "World's Fair," opened in London. The Exhibition was to be a celebration of progress in the arts, sciences, and industry. The plan was to send *America* to England to take part in the festivities and to be an example of Yankee shipbuilding.

Providing an example of Yankee shipbuilding wasn't all of it, however. *America*'s owners, who included John Cox Stevens, owner of the aforementioned *Maria*, his brother Edwin, J. Beekman Finlay, James Hamilton, and George L. Schuyler, hoped to win wagers with her. These early members of the New York Yacht Club were "sportsmen," a polite term for men who liked to place wagers on sporting events. John Cox Stevens, for example, by then a wealthy shipowner from Hoboken, New Jersey, once bet $20,000 on a horse race — and won. He was president of the prominent Jockey Club.

America *was designed by George Steers, unquestionably the preeminent designer of small vessels in the United States at the time. Steers also supervised her building at William H. Brown boatyard in lower Manhattan.*

Sportsmen or not, the Stevens family was one of the most notable in the short history of this country. The family controlled steamship travel in America. In 1804, when he was 19, John Cox Stevens had been the first to steer a propeller-driven boat. His father, John Stevens, invented steam engines and designed steamships. His brother Robert invented weapons and railroad tracks, and drew the lines for numerous steamships. His brother and fellow syndicate member Edwin would, upon his death, endow the Stevens Institute of Technology, whose campus would be established on the family estate on the New Jersey banks of the Hudson River. Here, many prominent America's Cup yachts would be tank-tested. Also on the family estate at Castle Point, in Hoboken, would be the first clubhouse of the New York Yacht Club.

America was designed by George Steers, who also supervised her construction. She was shaped along the lines of the Sandy Hook pilot boat. These were typically fast craft, designed to lead ships safely into port. *America* was a schooner, with her two masts raked sharply aft. She was about 95 feet long on deck, with a bowsprit projecting out 17 feet. She drew 11 feet and had a relatively narrow beam of about 23 feet. Distinguishing features were her very fine, concave bow, low freeboard, and simple sailplan.

America failed the aforementioned "test." She was beaten by the *Maria*, the Stevens family's 110-footer whose lines had been drawn by Robert Stevens. It was, to be sure, an unfair test as *Maria*, designed for flat water, was no sea boat. She had a centerboard rather than a fixed keel like *America*. Also, while the two boats were fairly similar in size, *Maria* carried 2500 square feet more sail than *America*. *Maria* required a crew of 55; *America* would sail the famous race that lay ahead of her with 21.

Other than *America*, this fledgling country's offerings at the International Exhibition were humble. Writing about America's pedestrian agricultural devices on display there, the London *Times* said, "If the Americans do excite a smile, it is by their pretensions..."

America sailed for France on June 21, 1851. She was, reportedly, the first yacht to cross the Atlantic in either direction. Syndicate members traveled to France by steamship to wait for their yacht. While in Paris, James Hamilton, the son of Alexander Hamilton, encountered Horace Greeley, the noted New York newspaper editor. Greeley warned him: "The eyes of the world are on you. You will be beaten, and the country will be abused, as it has been in connection with the Exhibition." Greeley strongly recommended that *America* avoid racing any British yachts. Hamilton replied, "We're in for it and must go."

The syndicate met *America* in Le Havre, France. After being provisioned, she sailed for the town of Cowes on the Isle of Wight, where Queen Victoria had a summer home, Osborne House. While approaching Cowes, *America* engaged the English yacht *Lavrock* in an informal race, easily beating her — something that was witnessed by hundreds ashore.

The Isle of Wight was and still is the home of the Royal Yacht Squadron, and the epicenter of yachting in England. The Royal Yacht Squadron, formed in 1815, was the first club in England to be granted the "Royal" designation. It has been described as the "most exclusive club in the universe." So exclusive is it that Sir Thomas Lipton, who challenged for the America's Cup five times from 1899 to 1930, was denied membership until he was 80 and very near his death.

By 1851, yachting had a 250-year tradition in England. "Britannia," which according to legend and song, "ruled the waves," had 800 yachts at the time. The tradition in America dated back only about seven years to 1844, when the New York Yacht Club (NYYC) was formed aboard *Gimcrack*, another John Cox Stevens yacht. While not the first yacht club in America, the New York Yacht Club would become this nation's most prestigious for many reasons, not the least of them being its 132-year stewardship of the America's Cup.

John Cox Stevens, who headed the America syndicate, was the first commodore of the New York Yacht Club. His grand-father was a member of the Continental Congress.

Upon *America*'s arrival in Cowes, several members of the Royal Yacht Squadron visited her. Among them was the Marquis of Anglesey, then governor of the Isle of Wight. After exchanging pleasantries, the Marquis said about *America*'s design, "If she is right, we are all wrong."

Stevens got to the heart of the matter. To his hosts he issued a friendly challenge to "any and all schooners of the Old World" for a race. After the success of *America* against *Lavrock*, this challenge was politely ignored, although Stevens and his crew were made honorary members of the Royal Yacht Squadron, a considerable honor.

When the British ignored *America*'s challenge, Commodore Stevens increased the stakes. He offered to race any yacht for "any sum from one to ten-thousand guineas." The British ignored this offer, too. The London *Times* attempted to rally what it described as

This castle became the home of the Royal Yacht Squadron in 1857, after the death of its owner, the Marquis of Anglesey. It was the Marquis, a member of the Royal Yacht Squadron, who said of America before the race, "If she is right, we are all wrong." After the race he said, "I've learned one thing. I've been sailing my yacht stern foremost for the last 20 years."

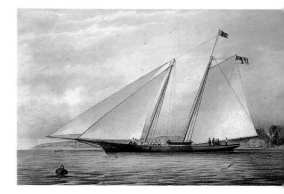

Someone talked Commodore Stevens into carrying a "flying jib" — the foresail set on a boom in this painting — for the race. Captain Dick Brown, America's skipper, was adamantly against the addition of this sail. When racing upwind to St. Catherine Point, the boom supporting the jib broke. Captain Brown said, he was "damn glad it was gone."

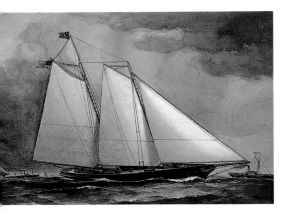

America's competition ranged in size from the 392-ton Brilliant to the 47-ton cutter Aurora (opposite page). America, pictured here, was in the middle at 170 tons. Rated tonnage in this case was a custom-house measurement, applied to determine tariffs. It shouldn't be confused with weight, or displace-ment. It is, however, indicative of relative size. It was Brilliant's owner, a Mr. Ackers, who filed the protest against America.

the "faint-hearted yachtsmen" of England to action.

As *America* waited for a race, her legend grew. James Hamilton wrote, "There was a very great impression among the lower classes... at Cowes that *America* had a propeller which was ingeniously concealed; and our crew amused themselves by saying to the boatmen who came alongside with visitors, 'In the stern sheets, under the gangway, there is a grating which the commodore does not allow any person to open...'"

It wasn't a propeller that made *America* faster, it was her shape and her sails. Pilot boats were fine forward, showed their greatest beam amidships, and carried their beam well aft. This, of course, is the normal shape of boats today. Most English yachts were wide forward and narrow aft, a shape that used to be described as "apple-bowed." The result was that *America* had a more easily driven hull than the English yachts. *America* also had new cotton sails, which stretched less and maintained their shape better than the traditional flax sails of the British boats.

While waiting for an appropriate race, Stevens had the good sense to enter a free-for-all on August 22 for the Hundred Guinea Cup. The race, "open to yachts belonging to clubs of all nations," was to be clockwise around the Isle of Wight. In addition to the 100-guinea cash prize (a guinea is worth slightly more than a pound), there was to be a silver trophy, 27 inches high, 36 inches around, and weighing 134 ounces. It was officially called "The Royal Yacht Squadron £100 Cup." Alternatively, it was known as the "Hundred Guinea Cup." This name did not represent the value of the trophy itself, but the cash prize that accompanied it.

On Friday, August 22, *America* sailed against 15 English cutters and schooners, ranging in size from the 47-ton cutter *Aurora* to the 392-ton *Brilliant*. *America* was in the middle at approximately 170 tons. In keeping with the custom of the day, the race started with the yachts anchored. *America* overran her anchor and was the last to start. The first leg was downwind in very light air, and *America*, with her easily driven hull, enjoyed the building breeze and caught the fleet. At the first mark, at Noman's Land buoy, she was fifth. The next leg was a reach, and *America* moved to the front of the fleet.

The usual course when racing around the Isle of Wight was to round the Nab lightship, about five miles from the eastern tip of the island. However, the printed instructions given to *America* only said that it was to be "round the Isle of Wight, inside Noman's buoy and Sandhead buoy, and outside the Nab." Thus *America* rounded a white buoy more than a mile inside the lightship; the other boats sailed the longer course. This later resulted in a protest.

It was on the 223-foot royal yacht, Victoria and Albert where the Queen learned that America was first and "There is no second." When passing the royal yacht, America's crew removed their hats and dipped their flag in a show of respect for the British monarch. The Queen took considerable interest in America. Visiting the yacht the next day, she even inspected the bilges and asked to see how the ballast was stowed.

This poster, by W. W. Yelf, printer to the Royal Yacht Squadron, announces the race America entered on August 22, 1851. The R.Y.S. £100 Cup was last on the regatta schedule.

Next came a 15-mile upwind leg to St. Catherine Point, then a reach to the Needles. There "the wind fell and the haze set in," according to the London *Illustrated News*. *America* led *Aurora*, her nearest competitor, by seven and a half miles. The rest of the fleet, according to the London *Times*, was "nowhere." At 6:00 p.m., 10 minutes after rounding the Needles, *America* neared the 223-foot royal yacht, *Victoria and Albert*. Aboard the paddle-driven steam yacht were Queen Victoria, Prince Albert, and the 10-year-old Prince of Wales, who would become King Edward VII in 1901.

A *deck scene aboard* Cambria, *the first challenger for the America's Cup, in 1870.* Cambria *was owned by James Ashbury, from England. Winfield Thompson described Ashbury as a man of great wealth; however, "his social standing was not high. His efforts to win the Cup were in the nature of a bid for social and popular favor." In short, Ashbury hoped to be elected to Parliament.*

T*his etching from* Harper's Weekly *shows* Cambria *crossing the ocean in a gale for the 1870 Cup match. For the transatlantic passage,* Cambria *raced* Dauntless, *owned by James Gordon Bennett, a member of the New York Yacht Club.* Cambria *sailed the 2917 miles in 23 days, five hours, and 17 minutes.* Dauntless *finished one hour and 43 minutes later.* Dauntless, *too, would sail in the first defense, a fleet race.*

Queen Victoria supposedly asked an attendant, "Who is first?" When told it was *America* she asked, "Who is second?" "There is no second," was the reply, or so the story goes.

America finished the race at 8:37 that evening. Then it was an anxious night waiting for the results of the protest stemming from the mark-rounding. The protest was disallowed.

The next day, *America*, at Queen Victoria's behest, traveled to her summer home, Osborne House. The diminutive Queen, Prince Albert, and various ladies and gentlemen in waiting went aboard the yacht. Before Prince Albert went below, Dick Brown, *America*'s captain, asked him to wipe his feet. The Prince paused in astonishment. Captain Brown said, "I know who you are, but you'll have to wipe your feet."

This Royal visit was the subject of conversation for weeks. It signaled a change in the English attitude toward Americans. As Winfield M. Thompson wrote in *The Lawson History of the America's Cup*, the friendly feeling Queen Victoria showed toward Americans in this critical period of this country's development was "of more benefit to this nation than the world knew." Instantly *America*'s victory became the stuff of legend, at home and abroad. The London *Merchant* wrote pessimistically that this win foretold a change in the world's order: "...The empire of the seas must before long be ceded to America... America, as mistress of the ocean, must overstride the civilized world."

The syndicate returned to America without the boat, but with an ornate if decidedly ugly silver urn. The Royal Yacht Squadron's Hundred Guinea Cup was passed around to the members of the America syndicate. When the surviving members of the group gave it to the New York Yacht Club, on July 8, 1857, they called the trophy the "America's Cup."

The syndicate drafted a simple Deed of Gift to govern the contest in the future. The 1857 Deed promised: "Any organized yacht club of any foreign country shall always be entitled through any one or more of its members, to claim the right of sailing a match for this cup... The parties desiring to sail for the Cup may make any match with the yacht club in possession of the same that may be determined upon mutual consent... The challenging party [is] being bound to give six months' notice in writing, fixing the day they wish to start. This notice to embrace the length, custom-house measurement, rig and name of the vessel." The Deed also said that the match should be "a friendly competition between foreign nations," and that the challenger had to travel to the competition "on its own bottom."

On July 21, 1857, the NYYC sent out invitations to yacht clubs around the world, promising a "spirited contest for the championship." This the America's Cup has usually been. The club also promised a "liberal, hearty welcome and the strictest of fair play." The issue of "fair play" is more complex, however, and would receive much attention, particularly in recent years.

INITIAL DEFENSES: 1870-1887

The first challenge was proffered by James Ashbury, from England, in 1868, for a match in 1869. Ashbury's father had grown rich after inventing a way to group multiple wheels on the undercarriage of railroad cars. Winfield Thompson, writing in the insightful *Lawson History*, describes James Ashbury as a man of great wealth;

however, "His social standing was not high. His efforts to win the Cup were in the nature of a bid for social and popular favor."

Ashbury challenged in his own right, with a complex list of conditions. The New York Yacht Club pointed out that clubs, not individuals, could challenge for the Cup, so Ashbury challenged under the auspices of the Royal Thames Yacht Club. Ashbury and the NYYC also tussled over the definition of the word "match" in the Deed of Gift. The word notwithstanding, the NYYC felt strongly that a challenger should face the same conditions as *America* had in 1851, in other words, a fleet race. Ashbury argued that a match meant one-on-one.

Further, Ashbury objected most strenuously to the use of centerboarders in the contest. The English disparaged centerboarders as "skimming dishes," whereas centerboard boats, like the Stevens brothers' *Maria*, made up much of the NYYC fleet. Finally, Ashbury objected to the course: this was the club's infamous "inside course" off Staten Island, in New York, which featured strong and idiosyncratic currents, moving sandbars, and considerable commercial traffic. Commodore Stevens had had little affection for the course he sailed in England in 1851, describing it as "notoriously one of the most unfair to strangers that can be selected..." The club took the attitude, therefore, that what had been good for Commodore Stevens in 1851 would be good for the challenger in 1870.

On all these points Ashbury was defeated, and his *Cambria*, which was 108 feet overall, met 17 boats from the NYYC on August 8, 1870. *Magic*, a small centerboarder of 84 feet overall, won the race. *Cambria* finished eighth, 42 minutes behind the winner. When the time allowance was figured (the America's Cup was sailed with a time allowance until 1930 and the J-Class era), *Cambria* dropped to tenth.

The first three boats in the race were all centerboarders. In fact, the New Yorkers' domination of this contest in the early years can be explained in large part by their use of centerboarders. Raising the centerboard when sailing with the wind aft of the beam reduces drag; when more lateral resistance is needed when sailing upwind, the board is dropped to its deepest position. Such movable appendages weren't considered safe at sea, however, and since a challenger had to travel to the competition "on its own bottom," according to the Deed, challengers were with very few exceptions keelboats.

The first defense of the Cup was reportedly viewed by 20,000 spectators. An estimated 65,000 people watched the America's Cup 25 years later, in 1895, more than watched baseball's World Series that year. One wonders how much more popular the America's Cup might be today if the NYYC hadn't moved the competition from New York and its "huddled masses," to Newport, with its more rarefied atmosphere, as it did in 1930.

Ashbury challenged again for 1871 with *Livonia*. Again he objected to having to race a fleet. This change the yacht club refused to consider. Then Ashbury countered cleverly: He would get a number of yacht clubs in England to challenge for the Cup; each would name his *Livonia* as the challenger. Then he would have the right to race the NYYC fleet 10 or even 20 times.

To settle the one-boat-against-a-fleet issue, the NYYC turned to George Schuyler, the sole surviving member of the America syndicate for an opinion. Schuyler minced no words: "It seems to me that the present ruling of the club renders the *America*'s trophy useless as a Challenge Cup; and that for all sporting purposes it might as well

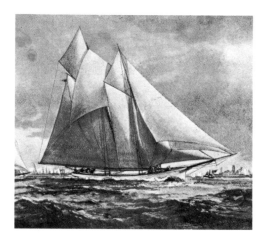

Magic, a small centerboarder, finished first in the first defense in 1870. Said one writer about this inaugural defense, viewed by 20,000 spectators, "When the Magic *rounded the lightship, making it almost a certainty that the Cup was safe, there arose a shout painful in its intensity of delight, for it was the relieved outcome of pent-up excitement which had reached its culmination at this very point."* Cambria *finished tenth in the fleet.*

The finish of the first defense off Staten Island. Shown here, from left to right, are Cambria *(the challenger),* Dauntless, America, Idler, *and* Magic *(the winner). There is considerable artistic license taken here as* Cambria *finished eighth, 42 minutes behind the winner. When the time allowance was applied,* Cambria *dropped to tenth. The first three boats in the race had centerboards rather than fixed keels. The old* America, *which then belonged the U. S. Naval Academy, finished fourth — the best finish for a keelboat.*

be laid aside as a family plate..." In a letter published in 1871 in the *Spirit of the Times*, Schuyler wrote, "A match means one party contending with another party upon equal terms..."

What Schuyler said was not what the NYYC wished to hear. While conceding this point, the club reserved the right to name a different defender on the morning of each race from a pool of four yachts. This would enable them to match the strengths of a particular boat to the weather and course.

While still in England, Ashbury made several additional demands, among them that the course be beyond Sandy Hook, outside the difficult waters of New York Harbor. The club finally offered a compromise: the races would alternate between the inside and outside course.

Ashbury wasn't in a compromising mood, however, and he challenged in the name of 12 yacht clubs. He was the commodore of one, the Royal Harwich, and a member of the other 11. Each named his *Livonia* as the challenger. When Ashbury reached America, he said, "My ultimatum is that all 12 races must be sailed, not only as a matter of right, but, I think, as an act of courtesy and consideration to me... A decision to reduce the 12 races will result in *Livonia* at once returning to England without any race..." This would be the first ultimatum sounded in the America's Cup, in 1871. It wouldn't be the last.

With the sailing season waning, Ashbury and the NYYC finally reached an agreement. The match would be the best of seven races; the races would alternate between the inside and outside courses, with the outside courses being 40 miles long and windward-leeward. The yacht club selected four boats to defend its honor: *Columbia* and *Palmer*, both centerboarders, as well as *Dauntless* and *Sappho*, both keelboats.

Columbia, 108 feet overall, won the first race on the inside course by 27 minutes on corrected time. She was named to defend again for the second race. She seemed a strange choice for the outside course, as a keelboat would have an advantage going to windward. However, the committee did not set such an upwind course; they laid it out as two reaches. This would favor a centerboarder like *Columbia*.

There was an ambiguity about which way to pass the turning mark. *Columbia*'s skipper, Nelson Comstock, asked the committee for instructions and was told to pass the mark on either side. This information, however, was never relayed to *Livonia*. In England, when no instructions were given, marks were to be passed to starboard.

Livonia won the start of the second race, and reached the turning mark, an anchored boat, two minutes ahead of *Columbia*. *Livonia* jibed around the mark, to keep it to starboard. It is no easy matter for a boat with big sprit-topsails aloft to jibe. By doing so, *Livonia* lost both speed and distance to windward. When *Columbia* turned the mark, she left it to port and merely tacked around it. This put her upwind of *Livonia*. Within a short time *Columbia* used this windward position to take the lead and eventually the race.

Ashbury protested, the first protest in the America's Cup. It, too, wouldn't be the last. Ashbury said *Columbia* had violated the sailing rules by tacking around the mark rather than jibing; also the race was to have been windward-leeward, not two reaches. Finally, rather

In the second defense in 1871, Ashbury again objected to a fleet race. New York compromised by naming four boats, including Dauntless (left). New York attempted to match its defender to the conditions.

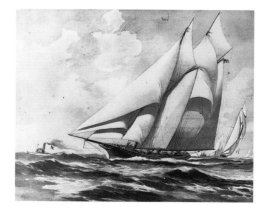

The *American defender* Columbia *leads* Livonia *in the protested second race. The instructions were not clear on how to round the turning mark.* Columbia's *skipper was told to leave the mark on either side. This information, however, was never relayed to* Livonia. Livonia, *ahead at the mark, jibed.* Columbia *tacked. This put the defender upwind of* Livonia. *From this windward position,* Columbia *took the lead and the race.*

Sappho, *a keelboat of 135 feet, won races four and five for the New Yorkers, making for a successful defense. Ashbury, however, didn't agree with the scorekeeping because of the protested second race. He showed up for race six, but New York refused to send an official representative. Ashbury then claimed the America's Cup for his own, but, of course, left for England without it.*

The Countess of Dufferin *was the first challenger from Canada, sailing in the third match in 1876. She was also the last schooner to challenge for the Cup.* Madeleine, *which beat her by 19 minutes on average, was, likewise, the last defending schooner.* Countess of Dufferin *was designed, built, and skippered by Alexander Cuthbert.*

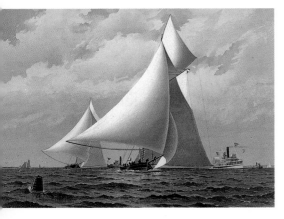

Mischief, *in the foreground, leads the Canadian challenger,* Atalanta, *in 1881 in the fourth defense. To get through the locks before entering the Erie Canal,* Atalanta, *more than a foot too wide, was reballasted so she heeled over and was pulled by mules. Even then, the boat's sides and bottom were badly scraped by the passage.* Mischief *beat* Atalanta *by 33 minutes on average.*

than the race being 40 miles, as specified, it was closer to 30. Interestingly, Ashbury didn't ask for the victory; he asked for the race to be sailed over. The committee didn't accept his protest.

In the third race, the committee again chose *Columbia*. This was a surprise to everyone, but especially the crew of *Columbia*. They had been told they would have the day off, and had been celebrating their two victories with considerable enthusiasm the previous night. *Dauntless*, however, which had been expected to defend, had rigging problems, as did the other two possible defenders, so *Columbia* sailed with a group of amateurs, including an actor.

While trailing in the race, *Columbia* suffered two breakdowns — one of her masts broke, and she lost steering. *Livonia* won race three by 19 minutes, 33 seconds; the time allowance would reduce that to 15 minutes. This was the first America's Cup race won by a challenger.

Sappho, a keelboat of 135 feet, won the next race, making the score 3-1 for the New Yorkers. By Ashbury's accounting, however, the score was 1-1, because of the protested second race. The next race *Sappho* also won, making the score 4-1, for a successful defense. Again, Ashbury didn't agree with the accounting.

Ashbury, not one to go softly into the night, announced that his yacht would be out the next day for race six. If no yacht met him, he would sail a windward-leeward course, and do it again the next day. When the NYYC did not send an official representative, Ashbury claimed the America's Cup for his own.

Ashbury left, of course, without the America's Cup. When he reached England, he accused the NYYC of "unfair and unsportsmanlike proceedings." If he ever returned to race again, he said, he would bring his lawyers and fight these battles in the courts. In a letter to the NYYC, he said that racing in America was not conducted on the same high moral plane that existed in England. The letter has been on display in the New York Yacht Club since 1871.

The result of this challenge was that the British lost interest in the America's Cup. For five years there was no challenge. Then in 1876 a challenge came from the Royal Canadian Yacht Club in Toronto. The prime mover in the syndicate was Alexander Cuthbert, a Canadian boatbuilder and yacht designer. The New Yorkers were overjoyed; to accommodate the yacht they waived the Deed's requirement of six months' notice so that the contest could be held that very year.

Perhaps the most salutary thing to come out of this challenge was that when the challenger asked that the match be between one defender and one challenger, the NYYC, in a compromising mood, approved the change. The challenger was *Countess of Dufferin*. At 107 feet overall, she was designed, built, and skippered by Cuthbert. She was the first challenger to sail with a centerboard; being a Canadian entry from the Great Lakes, she didn't have to come too far.

This was the first America's Cup to start with the boats not at anchor; the start was timed, as it is today. The Canadian yacht, a rough-hewn, unfinished vessel, lost two races to the defender, *Madeleine*, by 19 minutes on average.

Cuthbert returned in 1881 with the 70-foot *Atalanta*, the first sloop to challenge. The American defender was *Mischief*, only the

In only seven years of work as a yacht designer, Edward Burgess drew three Cup defenders: Puritan *for 1885,* Mayflower *for 1886, and* Volunteer, *for 1887 and 134 other yachts.*

second metal yacht constructed in America. *Atalanta* lost to *Mischief* by 33 minutes on average.

It was obvious that these one-sided affairs were not good for the America's Cup. When Cuthbert announced he'd keep *Atalanta* in New York for another challenge next year, the New Yorkers asked George Schuyler to rewrite the Deed of Gift.

A primary goal of the new Deed was to keep Cuthbert away. Schuyler did this in two ways: He said no losing vessel could return unless "some other [challenging] vessel has intervened, or until after the expiration of two years." More specifically, he banned Great Lakes clubs. A challenging yacht club, he wrote, must hold races on an "arm of the sea." This clause would prove troublesome to Buddy Melges and his Heart of America Challenge for the 1986-87 match in Western Australia. Melges, whose challenge was from the Chicago Yacht Club on Lake Michigan, had to prove to a court that the Great Lakes were an "arm of the sea."

The first Royal Yacht Squadron challenge was in 1885, when Sir Richard Sutton's *Genesta* sailed against *Puritan*, the first America's Cup design from Edward Burgess, of Boston. Burgess was a Harvard-trained entomologist who became secretary of the Boston Society of Natural History. He was a member and club secretary of the Eastern Yacht Club in Marblehead, Massachusetts, and an amateur yacht designer. When asked by a syndicate of Eastern Yacht Club members to design a Cup defender, he accepted, although his largest design to date was 38 feet. Nevertheless, *Puritan* was one of three successful Cup yachts Burgess would draw.

James Bell challenged with Thistle in 1887, in the seventh match, through the Royal Clyde Yacht Club of Scotland.

The fifth defense, between *Puritan* and *Genesta*, is considered the high-water mark in international sportsmanship in this particular arena. Before the start of the 1885 match, *Puritan*, the defender, on port tack, tried to cross *Genesta*, on starboard tack. The foul carried away *Genesta*'s bowsprit. As a boat on starboard has the right of way over a boat on port, the committee ruled *Puritan* out of the race. Informed by the race committee that all he need do was sail the race for the victory, Sir Richard declined. "We are very much obliged for the honor, but we came to race the Cup defender and cannot accept a walk-over." Sir Richard lost, 2-0.

For 1887, there was a challenge from James Bell of the Royal Clyde Yacht Club in Scotland. The challenging yacht was to be *Thistle*, designed by George Watson. The owner told the NYYC that *Thistle* would be 85 feet on the water. The New Yorkers started building *Volunteer*, a Burgess design, which would be 86 feet on the water.

Thistle was built in great secrecy. When she was launched, her keel was draped and hidden, in much the same fashion as today's America's Cup underbodies are shrouded in so-called "modesty skirts."

After *Thistle* arrived in New York, a diver, at the behest of the New York *World* newspaper, inspected her lines one night. The diver's lines, drawn in the newspaper the next day, had nothing to do with *Thistle*'s lines, and indeed very little to do with yacht design. When Bell was shown the newspaper representation, he laughed, "When the *Thistle* is dry-docked and her actual lines are observed, the owner of that paper will feel like shooting the diver."

The New Yorkers finally got an official look at *Thistle*'s lines when she was measured. There were bullets aplenty, but none aimed at any diver. *Thistle* was

I*n the fifth match in 1885,* Puritan, *the defender, on port tack, was hit by* Genesta, *on starboard, before the start. As a starboard-tack boat has right of way, the race committee told Sir Richard Sutton,* Genesta's *owner, that all he need do was to finish the race for the win. He declined to do that. Sir Richard was the first challenger from the Royal Yacht Squadron; his father and grandfather were also members of this august club.*

According to her owner, James Bell, Thistle *(above), the challenger in 1887, would be 85 feet on the water. The New Yorkers built* Volunteer, *which was 86 feet on the water. When measured,* Thistle *was found to be 86.4 feet. The New York Yacht Club was outraged by this error and seriously considered canceling the match, even though the time allowance could easily address this difference. In fact, the total handicap only amounted to about five seconds.*

Volunteer *was the fastest as well as the last defender penned by Edward Burgess. She beat* Thistle *in the seventh defense in 1887. Burgess, a Harvard-trained entomologist, was a member and secretary of the Eastern Yacht Club in Marblehead, Massachusetts, and an amateur yacht designer.*

I*n the eighth match in 1893, Lord Dunraven's challenger,* Valkyrie II *(above), lost to* Vigilant *(on the opposite page), the first Nathanael Herreshoff defender. A loss, perhaps, but* Valkyrie *was ahead in one race by more than 26 minutes when the time limit expired. In the final race,* Valkyrie *led before blowing out two spinnakers. She lost this race by 40 seconds on corrected time.*

discovered to be 86.4 feet long, rather than 85 feet, as reported by her owner. There was talk of canceling the match, even though the time allowance could easily address this difference.

The NYYC finally asked George Schuyler, age 76, for an opinion. Schuyler said, "Although the variation between the stated and actual load waterline is so large as to be of great disadvantage to the defender of the cup, still, as Mr. Bell could only rely upon the statement of his designer, he cannot, in this particular case be held accountable for the remarkably inaccurate information received from him..."

The show went on, and *Volunteer* won the first race by 19:23. Bell then hired his own divers to see if someone had attached some sort of sea anchor to his boat to slow it down. There was no anchor, and *Volunteer* won the next race by 11:48.

Another challenge from Scotland arrived shortly after the 1887 Cup, but the New Yorkers rejected it, saying it didn't conform to the new Deed of Gift. It couldn't, of course, because there had been no announcement of and indeed no work on a second rewrite of the Deed of Gift. What was apparent, however, was that the New York Yacht Club was losing control of its contest. Thus, the NYYC appointed a committee of five to confer with George Schuyler on the subject of amending the Deed of Gift. Later the club revealed just how new that Deed of Gift was. It was more than five times the length of the original Deed and, according to one writer, read like a "mortgage."

Wrote Winfield Thompson, "...Previously, the NYYC demanded six months notice of a challenge, now it wanted ten. The club demanded to know the name of the challenging vessel, its load-waterline length, beam at the load-waterline, beam on deck, and draft — these dimensions, then, could not be exceeded — as well as the type of rig." In essence, this was a demand that the lines of any challenger be submitted to the NYYC for study before any yacht was produced.

The result was a firestorm both abroad and at home. Said the American publication *Forest and Stream*, "The whole future of international racing was, and still is, in our opinion, centered on the question whether the America's Cup...is...to be raced for on fair terms, or whether it is in effect the private property of the New York Yacht Club, the privilege of competing for it being accorded foreign clubs as a favor and not as a right."

In defense of the dimensions clause in the 1887 Deed, Schuyler wrote, "The main reason we ask for the [dimensions] is to know what kind of a vessel we have to meet. I believe the challenged party has a right to know what the challenging yacht is like, so that it can meet her with a yacht of her own type if it be desired."

The Earl of Dunraven would in his two challenges display an "obstinate resistance." The 1893 defense, his debut, was the first series not to use the New York Yacht Club's infamous inside course.

Eventually, the NYYC acquiesced. In essence, it reaffirmed that disagreements could be settled by "mutual consent." It also said the rules used in the last three challenges were acceptable.

THE GREAT SLOOPS: 1893-1920

Peace, however, didn't reign in the land. Much of that had to do with the next challenger, Windham Thomas Wyndam-Quin, the fourth Earl of Dunraven. If Sir Richard Sutton's challenge from the Royal Yacht Squadron was a high-water mark, Lord Dunraven's challenges from that same club were nadirs.

Vigilant, *which defended the Cup in 1893 in the eighth defense, was the first of the so-called "Great Sloops." By way of comparison, Burgess's* Volunteer, *which preceded this era, was 85'10" on the water and 106'3" overall.* Vigilant *was about the same length on the water but 124 feet overall.* Vigilant *also carried 11,272 square feet of sail, some 2000 square feet more than* Volunteer. *Seventy men were needed to sail* Vigilant.

Defender *was the second Herreshoff boat to defend the Cup; this was for the ninth defense in 1895 against Lord Dunraven's* Valkyrie III. *Note* Defender's *extreme amount of sail area; in subsequent years, it would increase even more dramatically. After the first race, Lord Dunraven claimed* Defender's *crew added ballast to increase the boat's water-line length. In short, he accused the New York Yacht Club of cheating.*

Dunraven's father, a convert to Catholicism, had forbade his young son to see his Protestant mother. To that end, he bundled the boy off to boarding school in Rome. It was there that the future earl came to display what one writer described as an "obstinate resistance." That phrase accurately characterizes his two America's Cup campaigns.

Dunraven challenged first in 1889, but the details couldn't be agreed upon. In 1892 he tried again, naming *Valkyrie II* as his challenger. He said only that she would be 85 feet on the water. The NYYC accepted this lack of information, and the races were held in 1893. This was the first series not to use the infamous inside course. Dunraven's *Valkyrie II* lost to *Vigilant*, a Nathanael Herreshoff design, in three straight races. Nevertheless, his boat was ahead in one race by more than 26 minutes when the time limit expired. In the final race *Valkyrie* led before blowing out two spinnakers. She lost this race by 40 seconds on corrected time.

Vigilant was the first Nathanael Herreshoff America's Cup defender. There would be five others, establishing an America's Cup record. Nathanael Greene Herreshoff attended M.I.T., and worked as an engineer in Providence, Rhode Island, before joining his brother, John, in the Herreshoff Manufacturing Company in Bristol. They started by building launches and small steamers, but also excelled at designing and building fast racing yachts.

Herreshoff's *Vigilant* signaled the end of wholesome boats in the America's Cup. What followed were a series of boats described as "the great sloops," or less affectionately as "rule-cheaters" or "freaks." These one-masted sloops showed huge overhangs, which increased their waterline length, and thus their speed, when they heeled over.

N*athanael Greene Herreshoff designed a record six America's Cup defenders:* Vigilant *in 1893,* Defender *in 1895;* Columbia *in 1899 and in 1901,* Reliance *in 1903, and* Resolute *in 1920.*

There is a direct correlation between waterline length and speed: the longer the faster. Burgess's *Volunteer*, which preceded this era, was 86 feet on the water and 106 feet overall. Herreshoff's *Vigilant*, by way of comparison, was about the same length on the water, but 124 feet overall. *Vigilant* also carried 11,272 square feet of sail, some 2000 square feet more than *Volunteer*. *Vigilant* needed a crew of 70 to sail her.

Dunraven returned in 1895 with *Valkyrie III*. He lost the first race to *Defender*, another Herreshoff design, by more than eight minutes. After the race Dunraven told the race committee that the American boat had added ballast the night before and was now two or three feet longer on the water than when originally measured. Dunraven's evidence was that a drain hole that had been visible before the race was now submerged. He demanded that *Defender* be remeasured, and prior to that, a neutral observer be placed aboard to make sure the ballast wasn't removed.

The observer wasn't put aboard, but when the American boat was remeasured the next day, it was found to be the same length on the water. The offending drain hole had submerged, it was said, simply because the boom had been shifted to that side of the boat. Dunraven's cause wasn't helped by the fact that he sailed the race first before lodging his protest.

An estimated 65,000 people watched the 1895 America's Cup, most of them on hired spectator boats. As a rule, the hired captains were well-behaved and kept clear of the racing boats; others, however, when asked by the race organizers to remain off the course, would shout, "Who are you to give orders?"

In the second race, an out-of-position spectator boat forced *Valkyrie III* and *Defender* apart on the final approach to the starting line. *Defender*, to leeward, passed downwind of the spectator boat; *Valkyrie III* passed it on the windward side. Then the two boats converged again. *Defender*, as the leeward boat, had right of way. Meanwhile *Valkyrie*, apparently early for the start, bore off to avoid crossing the line before the gun. A collision was inevitable. At the last minute, however, *Valkyrie* luffed, turning away from *Defender* into the wind. This action caused her main boom to foul *Defender*'s starboard topmast shroud, which sprung from the spreader. Without support, the topmast curved ominously. *Defender*'s crew nursed her around the race course, losing by 47 seconds. However, the NYYC rightfully disqualified *Valkyrie*. Dunraven argued, in spite of the evidence, that his boat hadn't fallen off; rather *Defender* had improperly luffed and caused the collision. He also said the behavior of the spectator fleet was impossible and dangerous, and unless the committee could guarantee a "clear course," he would not race. The NYYC said it had no power to keep the course clear. Dunraven, showing that obstinate resistance, refused an offer by syndicate head Oliver Iselin to resail the race, saying this would be an admission that he was guilty.

For the third race, *Valkyrie* came out under jib and mainsail but without topsails. *Defender* took the start. *Valkyrie* crossed the starting line more than a minute and a half later. As soon as she crossed the line, her tiller was shoved over, and she returned to port. Dunraven had quit, and Americans and Britons alike were scandalized.

Rather than apologizing, Dunraven published in the London *Field* an article in which he accused the NYYC of fraud. The NYYC was not wrong or at fault in this particular matter; still the bitterness and embarrassment of the "Dunraven Affair" nearly killed off the America's Cup.

The Cup gathered dust until into the scene rushed Sir Thomas Lipton, a knight-errant if ever there was one. Lipton was born May 10, 1850, into humble circumstances, a tenement house on Crown Street, in Glasgow, Scotland. His parents were Protestant farmers who had fled Ireland with the potato famine. Eventually they leased a tiny store at 13 Crown Street, where they sold ham, butter, and eggs.

From a young age, Lipton knew exactly what he wanted, and that was to be rich. When he was 14 he came to New York with eight dollars in his pocket. He chopped tobacco in Virginia, worked rice fields in South Carolina, and in New York clerked at a grocery store.

He returned to Scotland in 1869 with a barrel of flour, a rocking chair for his beloved mother, and $500. He worked at the family shop on Crown Street. With his return, business improved. He suggested to his mother and father that it might be a good time for "extension." "Who knows," he argued, "but there may be a Lipton shop in every city in Scotland." Ultimately, there were 500 shops in Scotland, Ireland, and England.

In addition to the grocery stores, there were packing houses in America and tea plantations in Ceylon. In 1897, Queen Victoria knighted Lipton to honor him for his contributions to Princess Alexandra's Royal Dinner for the poorest people in England.

Wrote Winfield Thompson, "Lipton was unique in England, though his type was not uncommon in America. He was a rolling stone, farm-hand, longshoreman,

Tea and grocery-store magnate Sir Thomas Lipton challenged for the Cup five times, from 1899 to 1930. In 1898 Lipton purchased Erin, *a steam yacht, on which this photograph was taken. King Edward VII enjoyed visiting aboard* Erin, *which caused the King's uncle Kaiser Wilhelm, of Germany, to wonder why the King of England went yachting with his grocer.*

For Lipton the America's Cup was always just out of reach. The caption on this cartoon reads: "An English Proverb Illustrated. There is many a slip 'Twixt the CUP and the LIP(ton)."

laborer... Behold him then in 1897, England's foremost tradesman-prince, not the old-fashioned, staid, proverbial English tradesman, but a tradesman of the hustling strenuous Yankee brand."

Many believe Lipton's first challenge, in 1899, was encouraged by his friend the Prince of Wales, who would become King Edward VII. It was the 10-year-old Prince of Wales, you will recall, who watched *America* finish first in that race around the Isle of Wight in 1851. Edward VII was an enthusiastic racing sailor who perhaps wanted someone to erase the memory of Lord Dunraven. The King, it was said, turned to his friend, Sir Thomas.

Before Lipton left for his first America's Cup challenge, Joseph Chamberlain, the British colonial secretary, beseeched him not to strain relations between the United States and Great Britain. In hindsight this was gratuitous advice, because no one lost better than Sir Thomas.

Lipton's Shamrock II, *with the dark hull, sails against a revamped* Columbia *in the eleventh defense in 1901.* Shamrock II, *a design of George Watson, was the first America's Cup yacht to be tank-tested. The boat was considered faster than* Columbia, *but Charlie Barr was smarter and a better sailor than* Shamrock II's *skipper, Edward A. Sycamore.*

Charlie Barr skippered three Cup defenders, including Columbia, *above right, in 1899 and 1901, and* Reliance, *left, in 1903. Only Harold "Mike" Vanderbilt and Dennis Conner have equaled that record.*

Lipton's 1899 challenge was an anticlimax. Due to foggy weather and light winds, it took 13 days for one race to be completed within the time limit. In due time, Lipton's *Shamrock* lost three races by decisive margins to *Columbia*, a Herreshoff design considered one of the most beautiful boats ever built. *Columbia* was skippered by Charlie Barr, who would successfully defend the Cup three times from 1899 to 1903. Only two others have equaled this: Harold "Mike" Vanderbilt, in 1930-37, and Dennis Conner, in 1980-88.

Lipton's second challenge was in 1901. The match, again, was slow to commence, this time because an assassin had mortally wounded President McKinley in Buffalo. Lipton's *Shamrock II* sailed against a revamped *Columbia*. *Shamrock* lost the three races, but in 90 miles of racing she lost by only 5 minutes, 36 seconds on corrected time. *Shamrock*, in fact, was ahead until the final miles of each race.

Lipton's next challenge for what he called the "auld mug" was in 1903. For this defense Herreshoff drew *Reliance*, which was 143 feet overall, 90 feet on the water, and powered by 16,000 square feet of sail. Measured from the end of her boom to the tip of her bowsprit, she was 200 feet long , the largest boat ever to sail for the America's Cup. *Shamrock III*, which was 134 overall and 90 feet on the water, lost two races and then got lost in the fog in the third.

Lipton challenged for 1907 but on the condition smaller boats be used. He proposed that the Cup be sailed in yachts of about 110 feet overall and 75 feet on the water. The NYYC rejected this idea, as these boats were of "insignificant power and size."

In the letter of explanation to Lipton, the yacht club wrote that the trustee [NYYC] could not accept any challenge that purported to add any design limitations beyond those expressly stated in the Deed. In fact, the New York membership unanimously adopted a resolution stating, in part, that, "... No agreement should be made with any challenger which imposes any other limitations or restrictions upon the designer than such as is necessarily implied in the limits of water-line length expressed in the deed."

Lipton challenged again for 1914. Once more he asked that the competition be held in smaller boats. The NYYC said, in essence, that challengers didn't write the

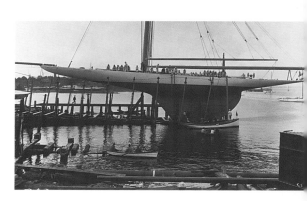

Reliance, which sailed in the twelfth defense in 1903, was the most extreme boat ever to sail for the Cup. Another design of Herreshoff's, she was 90 feet on the water and 143 feet overall. Measured from the end of her boom to the tip of her bowsprit, she was 200 feet overall. When heeled, the topsides became waterline, making the boat much faster.

The war suspended the America's Cup and led to much smaller boats when the competition resumed. The first post-war series was sailed in 1958 in 12-Meters, such as Columbia, which defended the Cup in the seventeenth match. Columbia was nearly 70 feet overall, 46 feet on the water, and had 1846 square feet of sail. Ranger, by way of comparison, the last of the J-Class yachts to defend the Cup in 1937, was 135 feet overall, 87 feet on the water, and showed 7546 square feet of sail.

the incident at the start, rendering his second protest meaningless, declined to hear both of Sopwith's protests on a technicality. It said he hadn't displayed his protest flag promptly. The race committee had wanted to avoid controversy but found itself in another firestorm. Said one writer about the incident, "Britannia rules the waves and America waives the rules."

Sopwith was incensed, and Sherman Hoyt believed his ire compromised his sailing after that. The final score was 4-2 for the Americans.

Harold Vanderbilt rewrote the yacht racing rules after this challenge. In 1934 he codified the International Yacht Racing Union (IYRU) rules, under which America's Cup contenders and practically all sailboats compete today.

12-METER ERA: 1958-1987

New York Yacht Club Commodore Henry Sears negotiated the change to 12-Meter yachts. This era spanned 29 years, from 1958 to 1987, and 10 defenses.

World War II halted the America's Cup. Then in 1956, after a 20-year hiatus, NYYC Commodore Henry Sears went to England to discuss with Sir Ralph Gore, commodore of the Royal Yacht Squadron, whether there was interest in continuing America's Cup racing in boats much smaller than J-Class yachts. This resulted in the 12-Meter era.

Two rule changes were significant. The Deed of Gift was amended to read, "The competing yachts or vessels, if of one mast, shall be not less than forty-four feet nor more than ninety feet on the load water-line." (Forty-four feet corresponded to the minimum waterline length of a 12-Meter.) The requirement that a challenger sail to the competition on its own bottom was waived.

The first post-war challenge was in 1958 between the defender *Columbia* and the challenger *Sceptre* from the Royal Yacht Squadron. *Columbia*, designed by Olin J. Stephens II, won easily.

Olin Stephens co-designed Ranger, which defended in 1937, Columbia in 1958, Constellation in 1964; Intrepid in 1967, Courageous in 1974, and Freedom in 1980. Stephens equaled Herreshoff's record.

For 1962 there came a challenge from Australia, *Gretel*, designed by Alan Payne. Payne tested models in the Davidson Tank at Stevens University, the institution, you will recall, that was endowed by Edwin Stevens of the original America syndicate. Payne also used American products, in particular sailcloth from the great American sailmaker Ted Hood.

Gretel, which sailed against *Weatherly*, designed by Phil Rhodes, proved herself the faster boat. However, like *Rainbow* before her, she was out-sailed by the American skipper, in this case Emil "Bus" Mosbacher. One result of this challenge, very close despite the 4-1 score, was that the NYYC forbade the use of American testing facilities and American products for challengers. They accomplished this through an interpretation of the Deed of Gift, applying a "country-of-origin" test on the design of a yacht, its designer, and its equipment. *America*, you will recall, had been "an example of Yankee ship-building," and this change returned the competition to its roots: The America's Cup would again be a test of a nation's technology and industry, as well as its sailors.

On December 7, 1962, the NYYC issued a memorandum saying that in the event it successfully defended the Cup in 1964, and, within 30 days, received more than one challenge for the next match, it would regard the challenges as "received

Gretel (the leeward boat), the first challenger from Australia, races Weatherly in the famous second race of the 1962 defense. Later in this race, Gretel would catch a private wave, generated by the 20-knot winds, and surf ahead of the defender, Weatherly. Gretel, built to the design of Alan Payne for Sir Frank Packer, is also seen on the opposite page.

winning streak in sports had ended.

How could it happen? After three straight campaigns, the Australians had recognized a fundamental truth: The America's Cup is a naval engagement, a test of men and machinery, as much as a war of words. For 131 years the NYYC had fought the battles on these two fronts better than any challenger. Challengers had had, on occasion, faster boats: *Shamrock II* in 1901, *Endeavour* in 1934, and *Gretel* in 1962 — but some link in the complex chain had been weaker. The Australians in 1983 were smarter than any challenger had ever been and smarter than the defender, on land and on sea. As Jeff Spranger, a journalist, said, "The Australians didn't answer the New Yorkers' questions, they mocked them."

The last America's Cup sailed in 12-Meters was, in some ways, the best. For 1986-87, the challengers traveled to windy Perth, Western Australia. If ever a boat needed

Stars & Stripes '87 *powers upwind in the winds of war in Western Australia. What with the "Fremantle Doctor," the name for the robust summer seabreeze, this the last match in 12-Meters was in some ways the best.*

Michael Fay challenged the San Diego Yacht Club in a boat that was 90 feet on the water. San Diego met the challenge in 1988 with the catamaran on the opposite page.

wind, it was the heavy, under-rigged 12-Meter. Also, the Cup seemed to benefit inordinately from the beautiful and somewhat exotic locale on the other side of the world. And television had discovered the America's Cup — cameras, mounted on the boats, at last showed spectators what sailing for the America's Cup was truly about.

When Dennis Conner's Sail America syndicate defeated the New Zealand effort, winning the right to challenge for the America's Cup, Malin Burnham, head of Conner's syndicate, received a visit from Arthur Santry, the commodore of the New York Yacht Club. Santry's message was to the point. According to Burnham, Santry said, "Since you people have a good shot at winning the Cup, I just want you to know, it still belongs to the New York Yacht Club." Burnham was stunned.

The America's Cup match of 1987 was between challenger Dennis Conner, representing the San Diego Yacht Club in *Stars & Stripes*, and *Kookaburra III*, from the Royal Perth Yacht Club, sailed by her Australian designer, Iain Murray. Conner won the match easily, 4-0, making himself the first man to lose the America's Cup and then win it back.

What 1983 indicated, 1987 proved: Multiple challenges had tipped the scales in favor of the challenger. In 1983, when New York lost the Cup, there were seven challengers from five nations against three defense groups. In 1986-87 there were 15 challengers from six nations against four defense teams. After 1987, it could be said conclusively that the road to the America's Cup runs through the Louis Vuitton Challenger Series.

THE CATAMARAN AND THE 90-FOOTER: 1988

While Conner won the 1987 America's Cup, the best record in Perth belonged to the New Zealanders, headed by Michael Fay, a merchant banker from Auckland. When Fay's *Kiwi Magic* met *Stars & Stripes* in the Louis Vuitton Cup, *Kiwi Magic*'s record was 37 wins in 38 races. Her sole loss was to *Stars & Stripes*.

Fay, however, was not one to go softly into the night. He proved to be an interesting combination of Lord Dunraven and Sir Thomas Lipton, showing both the obstinate resistance of the Irish Peer and the charm of Sir Thomas.

After his disappointment in 1987, Fay instructed his lawyer to read the Deed of

After Stars & Stripes '87 *(above) beat* Kookaburra III, *the defender from the Royal Perth Yacht Club, Dennis Conner and crew celebrate their 4-0 victory in the twenty-sixth match. Conner became the first man to lose the Cup and the first to win it back.*

Fay's huge monohull, New Zealand, which competed against Conner's catamaran Stars & Stripes in the twenty-seventh match in 1988 was constructed of carbon fiber and weighed an ultralight 83,000 pounds. By way of comparison, Ranger, the last and best of the J-Class boats, was 135 feet overall and weighed 332,000 pounds.

Fay's monohull, designed by Bruce Farr, depended to a large degree on crew weight to keep her from heeling too much. The crew, who numbered more than 30, perched on the wings.

Gift carefully. The lawyer, Andrew Johns, noted that the Deed still allowed challengers to sail in single-masted boats up to 90 feet on the waterline, as noted in the 1956 Deed amendment. On July 17, 1987, Fay gave the San Diego Yacht Club 10 months' notice of his intention to challenge in a boat 90 feet on the water. In one fell swoop, Fay took the prerogative away from the Cup-holder. Fay would dictate the size of the boat as well as the timing of the event.

It was clever in so many ways: The boat he proposed was on the edge of technology. Racing boats of this size — Fay's boat ultimately was more than 130 feet overall — hadn't been built since 1937 and the J-Class era. Also, Fay had a head-start in design; San Diego would be forced to explore new technology on the edge of yacht design with the clock ticking rapidly to the 10-month deadline. Further, Fay seemed to have more money to fund such a challenge than did San Diego, which was just getting used to the idea of being trustee of the America's Cup. Last, it would keep the spotlight on Fay, something he seemed not to mind.

It was, unquestionably, a sneak attack. That said, Fay's challenge was also completely legal, although it would take New York Judge Carmen Ciparick several months to make that determination. Two issues were argued before Judge Ciparick: the legality of Fay's challenge and San Diego's request to amend the Deed of Gift so that the defender would have the right to determine the type of boats to be used and the dates of the next America's Cup competition.

Arguing against SDYC's petition for the change to the Deed of Gift was the New York Yacht Club. This strange alliance, if that's what it was, between the NYYC and Fay's Mercury Bay Boating Club was, thinks Malin Burnham, the manifestation of Commodore Santry's warning in Perth that the America's Cup "still belongs to the New York Yacht Club." The NYYC's argument was also diametrically opposite to its December 7, 1962 memorandum that established the timing of the event (i.e. every three years) and the class of yacht (i.e. 12-Meters).

On November 25, 1987, Judge Carmen Ciparick ruled, "...Mercury Bay Boating Club has tendered a valid challenge..."

San Diego, for its part, hoped that Michael Fay would go away. When he didn't, San Diego commenced building two 60-foot catamarans, one with a solid wing sail, the other with a standard "soft" sailplan. A catamaran, San Diego reasoned, would be fast enough to beat what Fay was building; also it could be built in the limited time remaining. Further, San Diego conducted its own study of the Deed, done by Ed du Moulin and Harmon Hawkins, and concluded the catamaran was legal under the Deed of Gift, certainly as legal as Fay's 90-footer.

Fay returned to Judge Ciparick's court, where he sought contempt of court charges against San Diego for its decision to race a catamaran. The court ruled on July 25, 1988 that there was no basis at that time for a finding of contempt. The judge said, in essence, "Go race and come back later."

On September 7 and 9, 1988, Fay's huge monohull, *New Zealand*, met the wing-sailed, *Stars & Stripes '88*. The catamaran won both races easily.

The matter went back to court. New Zealand argued that a catamaran versus a multihull was an unfair "match," as that word was intended in the Deed of Gift; also that the defender was bound to compete on equal terms in a "like or similar boat." San Diego argued that the only design limitation in the Deed of Gift was that the competing vessel must be "propelled by sails only... [and] if of one mast, shall not be less than forty-four nor more than ninety feet on the load water-line." Its catamaran fitted comfortably within those two dimensions.

In ruling for Fay, Judge Ciparick concluded, "...The conclusion is inescapable that the donor contemplated the defending vessel to relate in some way to the specifications of the challenger."

Also persuasive were the following lines in the Deed: "This Cup is donated upon the condition that it shall be preserved as a perpetual Challenge cup for friendly competition between foreign countries." The judge determined that "the emphasis of the America's Cup is on competition and sportsmanship. The intentions of the donors were to foster racing between yachts or vessels on somewhat competitive terms..." So on March 28, 1989, Judge Ciparick awarded the America's Cup to the Mercury Bay Boating Club in New Zealand.

This was appealed twice: first, by the San Diego Yacht Club, and then by Mercury Bay. On September 19, 1989, a divided Appellate Division reversed Judge Ciparick's decision. Referring to the judge's previous decision, the Appellate Court wrote, "In finding that the vessels must be 'somewhat evenly matched,' the court promulgated a rule that is neither expressed in, nor inferable from, the language of the Deed..."

The court pointed to Schuyler's explanation of the dimensions clause, following the release of the 1887 Deed. Schuyler wrote, "... I believe the challenged party has a right to know what the challenging yacht is like, so that it can meet her with a yacht of her own type, *if it be desired.*"(Author's emphasis.) The court commented: "There can be no clearer expression of the intention of the donor that the defender was not required to meet the challenger with a similar vessel."

Also important was the letter the NYYC wrote to Lipton in 1907, explaining whose prerogative it was to select vessels: "...No agreement should be made with any challenger which imposes any other limitations or restrictions upon the designer that such as is necessarily implied in the limits of the water-line length expressed in the deed."

Fay appealed this, and the State of New York Court of Appeals concluded on April 26, 1990 that nowhere in the Deed of Gift had the donors expressed an intention to prohibit the use of multihull vessels or to require the defender of the Cup to race a vessel of the same type as the vessel to be used by the challenger. "In fact," wrote the court, "the unambiguous language of the deed is to the contrary."

The court also rejected Mercury Bay's contention that the phrase, "friendly competition between countries" connoted a requirement that the defender race a vessel of the same type or even substantially similar to the challenging vessel. Rather, the court saw the phrase "friendly competition between countries" as indicating a spirit of cooperation. "It was in this spirit of cooperation," wrote the court, "that the competitors had, since 1958, agreed to race in 44-foot yachts [i.e. 12-Meters]. Indeed, it was Mercury Bay, not San Diego, that departed the agreed-upon conditions of the previous thirty years. San Diego responded to Mercury Bay's competitive strategy by availing itself of the competitive opportunity afforded by the broad specifications in the deed."

The court returned the Cup to San Diego.

The Stars & Stripes *catamaran featured a solid wing sail, based on C-Class catamaran technology. The wing, designed primarily by David Hubbard and Duncan MacLane, was built by Scaled Composites in Mojave, California. Scaled Composites built* Voyager, *the airplane that flew nonstop around the world. The wing on the catamaran was 107 feet tall and comprised an area of 1860 square feet. It weighed 2000 pounds. Below, Dennis Conner, skipper of the catamaran, celebrates his victory.*

produces lift for quick acceleration, even at the expense of increased drag. In an automobile, it would be analogous to optimizing second gear rather than fourth.

To improve acceleration — or to optimize "second gear" — the shapes of the foils are altered. Variables include the sectional shape of the keel, where its maximum thickness is in the horizontal direction, its sweep-back angle, its length front to back, its depth, and the shape of the bulb on the bottom. The bulb, which contains 15 tons or more of lead, balances the sailplan and helps to keep the boat upright.

Other variables in appendages that allow a design to be more tightly focused include wings, as seen on *Australia II* in 1983; more radical keel configurations, such as the tandem keel; and the use, shape, and placement of the trim tab(s) on the back and/or front of the keel.

CARLO BORLENGHI

A technician works on an upside-down model used for testing by the Il Moro syndicate. The numbers on the model are helpful in pinpointing and measuring areas of lift and drag. Opposite is the hull, bulb, keel, and rudder of España. *This the most basic keel configuration is termed the "monoplane."*

DRAG AND THE HIGH-ASPECT-RATIO SHAPE

Drag comes in many forms. Two forms that a yacht designer is vitally interested in are wetted-surface drag and induced drag. Wetted-surface drag can best be described as the friction where a hull and its appendages touch the water. To decrease wetted-surface drag, yacht designers spend much time trying to diminish the chord length — or the fore-and-aft dimension — of appendages, such as keels and rudders. Induced drag, on the other hand, results from "leakage" over and often under a lifting surface. This leakage, from the high-pressure side to the low-pressure side, wastes energy. Increasing the depth of foils automatically diminishes induced drag.

Thus, the foils on racing boats have grown short fore-and-aft, to decrease wetted-surface drag, and deep, to decrease induced drag. The result is the tall and thin high-aspect-ratio shape — a veritable signature of racing-yacht designers and racing yachts.

WINGS

Wings increase draft, which increases lift and decreases induced drag when sailing to windward. Wings can also do this without increasing rating, which is clever: The draft limit in the 12-Meter, for example, where wings made their first significant appearance, is 9'2" (2.8m); beyond that there is a severe rating penalty. When *Australia II* was measured upright, her wings, which were angled down, didn't extend beyond this limit. As the boat heeled when sailing, however, the wings extended beyond the draft limit.

IACC boats, with their generous draft allowance of 13.12 feet (4m) and high-aspect shape, are less troubled by induced drag than 12-Meters. However, some of them, such as *Defiant*, *America³*, *Il Moro*, and *Stars & Stripes* (in the third round), sprouted wings. Upwind, wings could account for approximately a two-percent decrease in drag and a three-percent decrease in drag when tacking. A price was paid downwind, however, as wings increased drag by about one percent.

Wings not only serve to increase draft; like racing headsails that are cut low to touch the deck and prevent the escape of airflow, wings provide a similar "end-plate" effect that helps prevent the "leakage" of flow at the bottom of the keel.

While decreasing induced drag, wings, with their more complex structure, do increase wetted-surface drag. The net effect, however, is a decrease in total drag and an increase in speed to windward.

Today, America's Cup boatbuilders are faced with far fewer rules and employ a much higher technology. Consequently, America's Cup carbon-fiber boatbuilders have almost as much to do with winning or losing the Cup as do the yacht designers and technicians. For example, the failure of the rudder shaft on *Nippon* and her boom a few days later cost the Japanese two important semifinal races. Gear failure was not just a Japanese problem, however, as at least six masts toppled between the 1991 Worlds and the 1992 Cup competition.

Carbon-fiber boatbuilding is characterized by sandwich construction. The sandwich consists of two thin pieces of carbon-fiber "bread," strengthened by epoxy resin, and a honeycomb "meat" — typically made of an aramid (Kevlar) fabric — in the middle. Carbon fiber is one of the strongest and lightest building materials available; it is used, for example, in the construction of the Stealth bomber and Exocet missile. Strength-to-weight ratio is to a builder what lift-to-drag is to a designer — everything. The 2.5-mm (0.10 inch) carbon-fiber inner and outer skins are pre-impregnated with epoxy resin, which acts as a matrix, holding the fibers in position and working to glue the entire structure together. The very light honeycomb core, which adds stiffness, varies from 30 mm (1.18 inch) to 50 mm (1.97 inch) in thickness.

After being laid up over a male mold (built according to the designer's specified shape), the laminate is heated. Hulls can be cooked to 203 degrees F (95 degrees C). This hurries along the chemical reaction, causing the liquid-epoxy resin to change chemically and become a solid.

At the same time, pressure, in the form of a vacuum bag for the hull, or an autoclave for smaller pieces of the boat, pushes the elements of the sandwich together like a huge clamp or vise. An autoclave is a special oven that will withstand relatively high internal pressures for better compaction of the laminate, as well as higher heat. The IACC rule limits the hull to one atmosphere of pressure, or 14.7 pounds per square inch, attainable with vacuum-bagging — a fairly inexpensive method of pressurizing a material. The goal of the pressure is to compact the fibers and eliminate microscopic holes that weaken the structure.

Temperature is controlled in hulls to allow for the ordinary wooden frames in the mold. Above 203-degree temperatures, more fire-resistant materials would be necessary. Pressure is similarly limited in hulls to allow for vacuum-bagging. The reason for limiting pressure and heat in hulls is economic: There are few autoclaves in the world that can accommodate something 75 feet long and 18 feet wide.

Masts, booms, chainplates, rudders, keels, and other smaller parts can be baked and pressurized in autoclaves, however. The heat limit for these items is 288 degrees F (135 C), and the pressure varies from three to five atmospheres. Five atmospheres of pressure, as used on the rudder, is equivalent to 15 feet of lead over every square inch of the material. That's some clamp!

Carbon fiber has its strength in one direction, along the fibers; as such it is "orthotropic." In contrast, aluminum is "isotropic" — meaning it has equal strength in all directions. Therefore critical to the quality of the carbon-fiber laminate is the direction or directions in which the fibers are laid. This is termed "scheduling." A complex computer technique, called finite-element analysis, helps in this scheduling by calculating and modeling the stresses and strains encountered by the boat.

Two male molds are ready for the lay-up of the carbon-fiber inner and outer skins and a honeycomb core. The thin carbon skins provide the strength; the thick honeycomb provides stiffness. These wooden molds were constructed for the Italian syndicate, which built its hulls in two pieces. Most other groups built hulls in one piece. Opposite is the mold from the inside. The shapes come directly from the designers' lines.

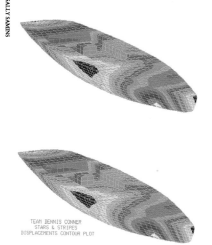

TEAM DENNIS CONNER
STARS & STRIPES
DISPLACEMENTS CONTOUR PLOT

An example of a finite element analysis done for Stars & Stripes. *Computer codes like this are used in the building of the boat. The black shades at the bow and keel show areas of greatest movement or deflection. This work was done for Team Dennis Conner by Newport News Shipbuilding.*

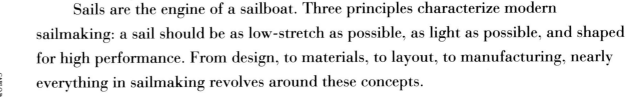

CARLO BORLENGHI

Montedison, the sponsor of the Il Moro syndicate, wove carbon-fiber into sailcloth with assistance from North Sails Cloth. The carbon fiber, which is black in color, was woven in one direction, with North's Gatorback Kevlar (the yellow, diamond-shaped threads) in the other direction. The carbon-fiber/ Kevlar was then laminated to Mylar.

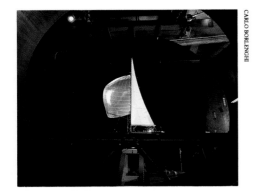

CARLO BORLENGHI

A *small model of a symmetrical spinnaker and a mainsail are tested in a wind-tunnel in Tokyo for the Nippon syndicate. Opposite, note the plethora of panels in the headsail. Computer-aided design and manufacturing now allow sailmakers to shape all the panels in sails. The result is a much smoother airfoil.*

SAILS

Sails are the engine of a sailboat. Three principles characterize modern sailmaking: a sail should be as low-stretch as possible, as light as possible, and shaped for high performance. From design, to materials, to layout, to manufacturing, nearly everything in sailmaking revolves around these concepts.

Low-stretch is important because it allows a sailmaker to lock in the designed shape. A sail that stretches in the wind is slow, out of control. Less obvious, a sail that stretches has a more limited wind range, which requires that crews change sails more often. This, like having to shift gears too often in a racing car, is slow.

Too heavy a sail can cause a boat to heel excessively. With lighter sails aloft the boat stands taller and is a better sail-carrying platform. In sailmaking, low stretch and light weight are addressed, primarily, in the choice of materials and in their lay-up. Most of the triangular sails on these boats — headsails and mains — were made of a Kevlar/Mylar laminate. Kevlar, which is stronger than steel for the same weight, is found in tire cord and bulletproof vests. Just as it is crucial to match carbon-fiber direction to the loads of a hull, it is critical to match Kevlar threads — which are also orthotropic — to the loads in a sail. To do this, sailmakers use their own version of finite-element analysis, or a "stress map," as they call it. In a triangular mainsail or headsail, major loadings run up and down the back edge, or leech, and radiate from the three corners or attachment points. Thus, the strong Kevlar threads are aimed down the leech and in radiating panels towards the center. This accounts for the typical tri-radial construction of these sails.

For 1992, carbon-fiber sails, as developed by Montedison and North Sails Cloth, and used on *Il Moro di Venezia*; and liquid-crystal sails, as developed and used by Bill Koch's America[3] team, were created for two reasons: they were lighter in weight and lower in stretch than Kevlar sails.

The design of a sail has to do, primarily, with its three-dimensional shape, similar to a keel. To give a two-dimensional piece of cloth a three-dimensional shape, sailmakers primarily use a process called "broadseaming." Here one side of each panel is cut with a curved edge, and its adjoining side is cut with a straight edge. When a curved panel is sewn to one with a straight edge, shape is forced into the sail.

There are as many as 120 shaped panels in a mainsail and 90 in a headsail. Sophisticated computer programs are now used to design and manufacture all these panels. Before the computer, a good sailmaker could shape a dozen seams at most. Computer codes can now shape all 120 panels of a mainsail. This provides a much smoother shape.

The sum of these pieces and thousands of others is the new IACC machine — as complete a test of a nation's technology and enterprise as there is in sports.

Robert Hopkins was technical coordinator and navigator for the Italian Il Moro di Venezia syndicate in 1992. Before joining the Italians, he worked for Dennis Conner in his successful 1986-87 and 1988 Cup campaigns. Comparing those campaigns to this one, he said, "I think that one of our secrets with Dennis was that we picked a few topics that we had to be perfect in and gave up on the rest. And we won by really picking our topics correctly. Now you have to be good in all of them."

AMERICA³ 🇺🇸 USA

It presumably doesn't take much skill to be born rich, as Bill Koch was. What matters is where you go from there, and William Ingraham Koch, who headed the America³ defense syndicate, has gone far. Like Lord Dunraven and Sir Michael Fay, Koch got there by brawling and waging war.

It was a sink-or-swim childhood in a competitive family. Koch's father, Fred, ran Koch Industries, a privately held oil business, which, according to the Wall Street *Journal*, is the "second largest closely held company in America." Fred Koch, who built oil refineries in the Soviet Union, among other places, was also a co-founder of the ultra-conservative John Birch Society.

Bill Koch, raised in Wichita, Kansas, spent a lonely childhood. "My parents were away a lot and left us in the care of others," he says. "There wasn't much love there, and what there was, we all had to compete for it." He and his twin brother, David, were the youngest of four children. Bill often found himself overshadowed by David and his older brother Charles.

As a youth, Koch was told by Culver Military Academy that he wasn't a good enough student to get in. He attended summer school there to prove he was, and eventually graduated third in his class. As a teenager, he spent summers working at his father's Matador Ranch in Quanah, Texas. He was, he said, more comfortable with the ranch hands than back home in Wichita. Koch was told by Culver Military Academy that he didn't have sufficient grades to get into the Massachusetts Institute of Technology. He got in and graduated in the top 10 percent of his class. He also played varsity basketball as a 6'4" forward. Koch was a reserve; he played behind his twin brother, who captained the team and was a small-college All-American.

Eventually, Koch received three degrees, including a Ph.D. from MIT in chemical engineering. His doctoral thesis was entitled, "The Flow of Helium Through Porous Glass." After joining the family business, he battled his brothers Charles and David for control. While he didn't win, the brothers paid him and another brother, Frederick, an estimated $650 million to go away. Today, Bill Koch runs the Oxbow Corporation, which sells thermal energy, produced in Nevada, to Southern California. *Fortune* magazine lists Koch's wealth at $650 million.

Koch has always been an avid sportsman. Once while white-water kayaking in the spring on the South Fork of the Salmon River in Idaho — a five-plus river in difficulty out of a rating system that goes to six — he flipped over and lost his paddle. In the spring runoff, the waves were more than 15 feet high. Without a paddle, Koch couldn't right the kayak. He came out of the tumbling, twisting boat and badly injured his knee. With this injury he swam a mile and a half through the rapids before he found a place to drag himself ashore. A day later he walked 15 miles to safety with a crutch he fashioned from a paddle. "That was the year I gave up kayaking," Koch said. He never gave up that tenacity, however — his dominant characteristic.

Koch started racing sailboats in 1984 with Ted Hood, in the Southern Ocean Racing Conference (SORC). It was there that he first saw maxi boats racing. Maxis are the giants of the International Offshore Rule (IOR); they are typically from 80 to 83 feet long and weigh from 75,000 to 80,000 pounds. Koch purchased a used 80-foot maxi,

Bill Koch launched four boats, including America³, *seen above. The boats were designed by the team of John Reichel, Jim Pugh, Doug Peterson, Jim Taylor, Dr. Jerome Milgram, and Dr. Heiner Meldner.*

BOB GRIESER

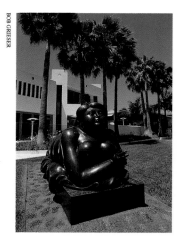

William Ingraham Koch, on the opposite page, led the America³ syndicate with a style all his own. This cigar-smoking nude from Koch's art collection decorated the lawn of his rented house overlooking the harbor and the San Diego Yacht Club. Koch's neighbors dubbed her "Roseanne."

Part of America3's *training included an early morning run on Mission Bay. To get his crew in shape, Koch hired the former trainer of San Diego's professional football team, the Chargers. Koch set a priority list of attributes for his crew: "Teamwork! Attitude! Sailing Ability!"*

A crewmember clears halyards on USA2, *an early IACC design that Koch purchased from the French. Koch built a total of four boats: Jayhawk, Defiant, America3, and Kanza. Throughout the trials, he raced two of them, like those seen on the opposite page.*

Huaso, which he renamed *Matador* after his father's Texas ranch. After a year of sailing with the professionals on board, he kicked them off and replaced them with friends. A lack of interest in "stars" would characterize his America's Cup effort, too.

For his second maxi Koch organized a design competition, the likes of which had never been seen before, in or out of the America's Cup. He asked 20 designers of varying reputations to submit lines for a new boat. These designs were tested in wind-tunnels, in a computer-driven velocity-prediction program (VPP), and in the test tank.

Koch also had yacht designer German Frers, most recently of the Italian Il Moro syndicate, submit the lines of six of his best-known maxis. Twenty-two-foot models were made from these designs, and they were rigged and ballasted as small boats. One of them looked like *Il Moro*, Raul Gardini's maxi; one looked like *Kialoa*, Jim Kilroy's maxi; one looked like *Ondine*, Huey Long's maxi; one was like *Boomerang*, George Coumantaros's maxi; and one was like Koch's *Matador*. These models were tested extensively. Then Koch invited the respective owners to his summer house in Osterville, on Cape Cod in Massachusetts, to sail the models of their boats in a regatta. "The model boats took on the personalities of their owners," said Koch. "Huey Long's ran aground; Jim Kilroy was fussing about the rules; Raul Gardini had an improper start." Koch, sailing the model of his first *Matador*, won.

Eventually Koch built *Matador²*, from the design of Bill Cook, Buddy Duncan, Penn Edmonds, and Dr. Jerome Milgram — an amalgamation of yacht designers and technicians, none of them a household name. *Matador²* won the Maxi Worlds in 1990 and 1991.

Doug Peterson, above, was a preeminent yacht designer in the 1970s. He was one of six designers and technicians who worked for Koch in 1992.

The technology Koch used in the building of *Matador²* was most impressive. Koch was, he says, approached by every American defense syndicate — at one point there were nine of them — looking to incorporate that technology in their 1992 Cup efforts. However, rather than be an accessory to the event, Koch decided to make his own attempt. He hired yacht designers John Reichel, Jim Pugh, Doug Peterson, and Jim Taylor, and technicians such as Dr. Jerome Milgram, a professor at MIT, and Dr. Heiner Meldner, a physicist at the Lawrence Livermore National Laboratory of the University of California, to begin work on a series of IACC designs.

Koch called his syndicate America³, as in "America cubed," or to the third power. The team became known as "the Cubens." The first boat was built by Hercules Aerospace in Utah; the last three were built by Eric Goetz of Goetz Custom Marine in Bristol, Rhode Island. Goetz also built Dennis Conner's IACC boat.

There were no individual "stars" dominating Bill Koch's America's Cup effort. Koch's attitude was embodied in the invocation, "Teamwork! Attitude! Sailing Ability!" And in that order.

It was different in the beginning. Early on Koch hired Gary Jobson, a television commentator on ESPN. Jobson, who had been tactician for Ted Turner in the 1977 defense of the Cup, eventually departed Koch's team, formally to "return to his other love, television." While Koch wouldn't comment specifically on Jobson's departure, he said, "The notable people who left the program all wanted me to pick the first team and put them on it. I said that I'm not going to do it that way."

Steering his own boat was, apparently, what he wanted to do, even though he'd only sailed for eight years. Koch took considerable heat from the press for this, who seemed to be more comfortable with non-sailing syndicate heads. To Koch, however, the nay-saying must have conjured up echoes of the administration people at Culver Military Academy, and he persisted at the helm.

Koch actively tried to diminish the mystique of the man at the wheel. "The people who have elevated steering have their own agendas. I view steering like any other job on a boat..."

The truth is, Koch had stars, but they were stars without overblown egos. There was, for example, Koch's chief helmsman, Buddy Melges, age 62, who had won the Mallory Cup, the U.S. Men's Sailing Championship, in 1959 and 1960; a bronze medal in the Flying Dutchman class in the 1964 Olympics; a gold medal in the Soling Class in the 1972 Olympics, and two World Championships in the Star class. Melges won his first Star Worlds when he was 48. In 1986, Melges skippered *Heart of America* in the America's Cup when he was 56.

Buddy Melges has a lifetime of impeccable credentials in the sport, including an Olympic gold medal.

The "Cubens" watch one of their boats perform. On the opposite page, Bill Koch, standing, steers. Said Koch, "There are two places where there's brilliance in an America's Cup program: One is in the tactics... The other is in conceiving the whole program... If I had enough experience, I'd be the tactician, but I don't, so I've taken a job where I can apply some manual skills."

This man, who has been sailing for 55 years, is the eternal flame of yacht racing. If the America's Cup were baseball, Melges would be Nolan Ryan. If it were golf, he'd be Jack Nicklaus. Such comparisons are deficient, however, because Melges is unique; a commingling of grandfatherly charm, youthful exuberance and innocence, charisma, vinegar, a large sense of humor, a faith in the old-fashion virtues, and decency. Melges, who raises dogs, is like an eight-year-old bulldog: He is mature and composed, loyal to friends — but still has a lot of bite when challenged.

For tacticians, Koch and Melges selected David Dellenbaugh and Andreas Josenhans. Dellenbaugh, the marketing director of North Sails Group Inc., was Melges's tactician on *Heart of America*. Josenhans, loft manager of North Sails East, sailed with Melges in his two Star World Championships. When Koch, in the late March, announced his first-string team, Josenhans moved to mainsheet trimmer.

After sailing the first race in the 1991 IACC World Championship, which was quite windy, Bill Koch told the press at a news conference, "I think the guys that made up the rule that designed these boats are idiots." However, he learned and grew with his challenge. A year later a much more composed Koch said, "These are great boats to sail — *if* you aren't paying the bills."

Koch paid at least $35 million of those bills. His corporate donors included Corvette, Coors Light, Digital Equipment Corp., Ralph Lauren, and Hercules Aerospace, Inc., which built his first boat.

When it was pointed out that his approach was very different from that of the other defense syndicates, Koch said, "I love it being different. I conceived of this program in my *Matador* days. I had a lot of rock stars aboard, and the boat was going slowly. I said this isn't working. It may work for someone else, but it isn't working for me. I'll conceive of a program based on what I think works..."

David Dellenbaugh, above, was one of two tacticians who sailed for Koch. Dellenbaugh was tactician for Buddy Melges in the 1986 America's Cup. In 1991 Dellenbaugh won the Lightning Worlds and the Thistle North Americans. He is an International Yacht Racing Union (IYRU)-certified judge.

TEAM DENNIS CONNER ▦ USA

Only one man in sailing could name his America's Cup team after himself with no one around him batting an eyelash, and that, of course, is Dennis Conner. Conner is in another orbit. *Business Week* called him a "sailing superstar."

Dennis Conner often says that he is not the world's best sailor, so he tries harder. Like much of what Dennis Conner says, there is more to this than meets the ear. The truth is, if one were to look at Conner's career in the aggregate, he *is* one of the world's best sailors *and* he tries harder. That, as many a competitor has learned, is a devastating combination.

In addition to two Star World Championships, Conner has won two Congressional Cups, which at the time was considered the World Series of boat-on-boat match racing. He has won four Southern Ocean Racing Conference (SORC) titles and an Olympic bronze medal in the Tempest class. He has been Yachtsman of the Year in the United States four times. In 1991, at age 48, he won the Etchells Worlds in San Francisco Bay. The 30-foot Etchells is, like the Star, a bellwether design.

Stars & Stripes *was designed by the triumvirate of David Pedrick, Alberto Calderon, and Bruce Nelson. Pedrick and Nelson worked for Conner in 1987, when his* Stars & Stripes '87 *regained the Cup in Western Australia. Calderon shaped the innovative* USA *for Tom Blackaller. Chris Todter was the technical coordinator for Conner's effort in 1992.*

Tom Whidden, above, has long been Dennis Conner's tactician and sailmaker. Dennis Conner, opposite, and Whidden have sailed together in every America's Cup since 1980.

In Australia, he is known as "Big, Bad Dennis." That is said with the utmost respect; to the Australians Dennis Conner is a worthy adversary. In this country, however, Conner's image is more controversial, at least to the media. Here, there seems to be a "tall-poppy syndrome" — a need to chop down someone who has grown taller than the rest. Conner is unapologetically a tall poppy; his success is something he's earned, not merely a gift of the gods.

In Conner, there is a focus and energy that is blinding in its intensity. Conner's long-time trial-horse skipper and fellow America's Cup sailor Jack Sutphen tells this story: "When we got to Hawaii, where we trained in preparation for the 1987 America's Cup, Dennis, Tom Whidden, and I sat down with a group of local businessmen. This man is telling Dennis that he owns a large department store, and he's going to devote an entire floor to the America's Cup. There will be pictures of the *Stars & Stripes* team training there, he tells us. It was all very nice. Right in the middle of this, Dennis turns to Tom and says, 'Tom, I've been thinking about the rudder. If we make that rudder four inches deeper and an inch narrower we'll get more speed.' The guy turns to me and says, 'I have never seen anything so rude in my life.' Such a focus doesn't make Dennis the most popular guy in the world, but it has helped to make him the best at what he does."

Conner was the first man to lose the Cup — and also the first to win it back. Here in a parade in San Diego, Conner displays the famous trophy, which dates back to 1851. Showing a thumbs-up salute is Malin Burnham, who ran Conner's syndicate in 1987, the year Conner brought the trophy and the match to San Diego. Burnham was president of the America's Cup Organizing Committee (ACOC) in 1992.

"It's not that Dennis is impolite," says his wife, Judy, an elementary school teacher in San Diego. "It's just that he's busy." It is sailing and the selling of his sailing projects — these days not necessarily in that order — that take up his time. His work day begins at 5 a.m. and often ends at 11 p.m. According to American Airlines, a Team Dennis Conner sponsor, he has flown 4.5 million miles in the last 10 years; that is 181 times around the world. Factoring out his bonus miles, Conner flies about 1000 miles every day.

Malin Burnham, president of the America's Cup Organizing Committee (ACOC), said, "Dennis has a greater combination of mental and physical energy than anyone I know. The meaningful, productive hours per day that he can devote to something is truly extraordinary."

They first met when racing on Ash Bown's 40-foot Owens cutter, *Carousel*, to Acapulco. Said Burnham, "There were five of us on board, including Dennis, who was 14 or 15. It was the first time that this group had ever sailed together, the first time any of us had raced overnight. This kid Conner never wanted to cleat anything; always wanted to make adjustments in sailtrim. In those days you'd adjust something and then wait 30 minutes to see if it was correct. But Dennis wanted to do it now. He tried to goad us older guys into action. We nicknamed him SAK, the smart-ass kid. That stuck with him for a long time."

KIRK SCHLEA

Stars & Stripes was christened in the spring of 1991. She was the oldest boat in the 1992 America's Cup fleet.

Losing the America's Cup in 1983 proved good for Dennis Conner. First, it rekindled his competitive urges, as he sailed off with a renewed focus and energy to clear his name. Second, winning the Cup back turned him into a star. Similarly, many believe that Conner's loss, and the sound and fury surrounding the legality of the winged keel, and those seven extraordinary races in September sparked new international interest in the competition itself: It was only when America lost the Cup that the rest of the world discovered it.

BOB GRIESER

David Pedrick of Newport, Rhode Island, was one of three yacht designers who worked for Conner. Stars & Stripes (right) power-reaches in a trials race.

"It could be argued that losing the Cup was the best thing that ever happened to me," said Conner, "as I took advantage of some of the opportunities that presented themselves when I won it back. But I didn't plan on losing the America's Cup, and then going to Perth to win it back, so that I could make a million bucks. In fact, if I had to do it again I absolutely wouldn't lose the America's Cup. Since I was 11, I've wanted and worked toward one thing: to be the world's best sailor, not its richest man."

Conner emphasized this statement with a keen (perhaps sharply pointed) sense of humor when he rented a waterfront house a few doors away from Bill Koch's rented estate during the 1992 America's Cup. Koch had brought with him a large part of his art collection, including three large bronze statues to decorate his lawn overlooking the harbor. One, a Rubenesque reclining nude by the Colombian artist Botero, is smoking a cigar. Koch's neighbors dubbed her "Roseanne" after TV star Roseanne Barr. Uniformed guards protected the collection 24 hours a day.

Not to be outdone, Dennis Conner placed on his lawn two raggedy-looking lions made of wood, unenthusiastically and unskillfully painted to look like bronze. If anything, Conner's lions needed more protection from the elements and gravity than from thieves.

The difference between Conner's one-boat program and Koch's four-boat program was as striking as the difference between their displays of art.

Stars & Stripes was designed by David Pedrick, Alberto Calderon, and Bruce Nelson. Conner's corporate sponsors included Cadillac Motor Car Division, Diet Pepsi, American Airlines, Citizen Watch, Televisa ECO, and Kodalux.

BOB GRIESER

The crew of Stars & Stripes adds its weight to the weather rail. On the following spread, a Bob Grieser photograph, are Stars & Stripes grinders (left to right) Hal Sears, Woodii Carr, and Jim Kavle.

IL MORO DI VENEZIA ■ ■ ITALY

To understand Paul Cayard, the 33-year-old American skipper for the Italian Il Moro syndicate, you have to understand the late Tom Blackaller. And to understand Blackaller, you have to understand Blackaller's relationship to Dennis Conner. From the Star class to the America's Cup, where they competed, Blackaller and Conner were, in terms of their personalities, polar opposites. These two came to greatness from very different directions: Conner through his talent and work ethic, Blackaller through his talent, charisma, and devil-may-care attitude. Conner and Blackaller were also ferocious rivals.

Cayard, while modeling himself after Blackaller, has some Conner in him, too. Said Cayard, "Tom, I think, was more of a natural sailor, and I think that's one of my strengths. I think, however, I'm technically much more involved than Tom was in the boats, about design — and I have a much higher tolerance for practice and testing, which are attributes of Dennis."

The five Il Moro*s were designed by German Frers, best known as a maxi-boat designer. Robert Hopkins served as technical coordinator for the project. Hopkins formerly filled that role for Dennis Conner in the 1987 and 1988 Cups.*

Paul Cayard was skipper of Il Moro di Venezia. *Cayard sailed on* Defender *in the 1983 Cup and on* USA *in 1987. Left is* Il Moro 1 *in Venice — her home port.*

Cayard started sailing when he was eight. At age 12 he reached the semifinals of the Sears Cup, the U.S. National Junior Sailing Championship. That success brought him notice from the St. Francis Yacht Club, the prestigious San Francisco yacht club under the Golden Gate Bridge. The club was, says Cayard, always on the look out for good junior talent.

The St. Francis Junior Program was like a farm team for future champions. Besides Cayard, many of the sport's luminaries trained there, including John Bertrand, silver medalist in the 1984 Olympics, who sailed for Dennis Conner in 1992. The club gave its junior members an old van with a trailer, assorted Laser dinghies, and a credit card. They went for weekend races up and down coastal California. Said Cayard, "That truck was incredible, and the trips were incredible. We used to sleep nine or ten to a room; we could only afford one room. A good spot to sleep was in the bathtub. That way there wouldn't be people tripping over you all night long."

In 1978 there was a match-racing event at the Balboa Yacht Club. Cayard was invited to participate. "I conned Tom Blackaller, who I'd met once, into teaching me how to match-race," he said. "That was really nice of him. Blackaller was a big deal at the St. Francis Yacht Club; he'd just opened the North Sails loft in San Francisco. I was basically an unknown, just another junior kid hanging around."

The crew on Il Moro di Venezia 3 *celebrates its victory in the IACC World Championship in May, 1991. The New Zealand boat finished second in the Worlds.*

Blackaller was, in truth, bigger than life. He was movie-star handsome and exuberant. He raced sailboats and automobiles. He rarely looked before he leaped into controversy. Despite a generation of difference in their ages, a great friendship developed between Blackaller and Cayard.

Blackaller planned to sail the Star North Americans in Toronto. When his crew was unable to make it, Blackaller told Cayard that if he was willing to trailer his Star to Toronto, he could crew for him. While waiting for Blackaller to arrive, Cayard and Craig Healy, another junior sailor from St. Francis, encountered Buddy Melges. Melges, from Lake Geneva, Wisconsin, warned the Californians about sailing on the Great

The launching of Il Moro 1 was a grand occasion in Venice. The photo above shows intramural action between Il Moro 1 and Il Moro 2.

Lakes. Said Cayard, "He told us, 'If you see a big black cloud coming toward you, that means we're going to get a squall. So get your sails down early because when that thing hits, it'll be blowing 50, and you'll sink before you know it.'"

When practicing, Cayard and Healy found themselves amongst Melges, Ding Schoonmaker, and Durward Knowles — all Star-class luminaries. Recalled Cayard, "I said, 'We're killing them!' Then a dark cloud comes, and it starts hailing. I think this must be what Melges is talking about, so I tell Healy to drop the sails. When it finally clears, there's nothing left except some life jackets and two guys bobbing about 100 yard away. One of them was Melges."

Il Moro di Venezia 3 *emerges from an airplane in San Diego. There would be a total of five boats built by Tencara Shipyard.*

After Cayard graduated from college, Blackaller landed him a job at North Sails San Diego, selling one-design sails. Cayard's parents were skeptical about a career in sailing, but Blackaller counseled that professional sailboat racing was about to become a viable career. Around this time, Cayard got a call to sail in Italy on a boat called *Nitissima*, an IOR 50-footer. His decision to go to Italy turned out to be pivotal: He placed second in the Sardinia Cup, and this success, in turn, brought him to the attention of Raul Gardini, then head of the huge Gruppo Ferruzzi chemical and agribusiness in Italy.

German Frers, designer of the five Il Moros, *was born and raised in Argentina. He learned his craft from his yacht-designer father and later at Sparkman & Stephens (S&S) in New York.*

Gardini was then racing a 67-footer named *Il Moro di Venezia*. Gardini invited Cayard to race on the boat. Under Cayard's command, *Il Moro* won two of five races, and Gardini was impressed.

In the 1983 Cup, Cayard sailed with Tom Blackaller on *Defender*, with little success. They teamed up again for the 1986-87 Cup, and this time did quite well, losing the semifinals to Blackaller's archrival, Dennis Conner.

When Raul Gardini decided in 1988 to make a run at the America's Cup, he asked Cayard to be his helmsman. At that point Gardini still ran the Ferruzzi empire, part of which is Montedison S.p.a., the largest chemical concern in Italy. To build the five *Il Moro*s, designed by German Frers, Montedison formed Tencara Shipyard, in Venice, and Montedison provided most of the materials and the technology. Today, Gardini is president of Gardini S.r.l., which has a controlling interest in Société Centrale d'Investissements, one of the largest financial concerns in France.

Raul Gardini, the prime mover in the Italian syndicate, relaxes on his Feadship, Tender del Moro. *Paul Cayard began racing with Gardini in 1985 aboard Gardini's* Il Moro di Venezia II, *a 67-footer. In 1988, they won the Maxi Worlds together on* Il Moro di Venezia III.

The Star class was important to Cayard — one reason was because it was important to his mentor and best friend, Tom Blackaller, who won the Worlds in 1974 and 1980. When sailing the Star Worlds in 1989, Cayard, who had won his first Star Worlds the year before, was in a restaurant with a friend. As Cayard recalled, "Someone walked in and said that Tom Blackaller had died of a heart attack while auto racing. I just looked at this guy and demanded, 'What are you talking about?' He asked me if I knew Tom. I said, 'Yeah, I know Tom...'"

There are people who have so much life in them, it is impossible to imagine them as dead. Asked if this America's Cup would have been sweeter with Blackaller around, Cayard said, "Yes. I think Tom would have been proud of me. My parents are very proud of me, and that's important, but they don't understand sailing. They don't understand the difficulty of doing an America's Cup the way Tom would have. I also had plans for him to help us, and he would have loved that."

THE NEW ZEALAND CHALLENGE NEW ZEALAND

Four diverse men — Sir Michael Fay, a New Zealand businessman living in New Zealand; Bruce Farr, a New Zealand yacht designer living in America; Peter Blake, a New Zealand sailor who has raced around the world four times; and Rod Davis, an American sailor living in New Zealand — defined the New Zealand challenge for the Mercury Bay Boating Club.

New Zealand is a lonely island nation with 3.5 million people and 60 million sheep. It tends to view the world through a David-and-Goliath perspective. New Zealand is also mad for sailing. There, sailing is front-page stuff.

Sir Michael, who has headed the New Zealand challenge since its debut in 1986, is an investment banker, not a sailor. In 1983 he watched with interest as *Australia II*'s victory galvanized that country and opened any number of doors for Alan Bond, the Australian businessman who had organized the challenge.

The fourth New Zealand boat, designed by Bruce Farr, was the most radical boat in the series. It was light and long on the water, with diminished sail area.

In 1986, when other Kiwi efforts to challenge for the Cup in nearby Western Australia foundered, Fay gathered the reins for his home country. In an extraordinary debut Fay's team came close to winning the Cup in Perth. Fay's 12-Meter *New Zealand*, also known as *Kiwi Magic*, went 37-1 in the capable hands of Chris Dickson before meeting Dennis Conner in the finals of the Louis Vuitton Cup. Sailing at her peak, *Stars & Stripes*, with Conner at the helm, won that contest 4-1. It is safe to say that if Conner hadn't stood in his way, Michael Fay would have won the America's Cup in his first outing.

Fay returned sooner than anyone expected. His attempt to challenge for the Cup in a boat 90 feet on the waterline in 1988, and the subsequent court battles that saw the trophy awarded to him and finally taken away again in 1990, have been chronicled in the history chapter of this book. It was a strange period in Cup history: If Conner was the first man to lose the Cup and then win in back, Fay was the first man to win the Cup and then lose it twice. And do so without winning a race.

For Fay, however, not all of 1990 was bad. That year Queen Elizabeth II knighted him, "For service to banking and yachting."

New Zealanders, in large and small sizes, conduct a challenge ceremony before the start of the Louis Vuitton series.

If Michael Fay had been charming and accessible in 1988, Sir Michael was strangely quiet for 1992 as if he had decided to let his boats do the talking.

Fay had naval architect Bruce Farr shape four Kiwi boats for his 1992 Cup

Bruce Farr designed the four New Zealand boats. Farr has been the one constant in Sir Michael Fay's three runs at the America's Cup.

challenge. Bruce Farr, who designed Fay's behemoth *New Zealand* for 1988 and worked as one of three designers for Fay's 1986-87 challenge, has lived in Annapolis since 1981. He was born in Auckland in 1949. His father, a printer who became a commercial fisherman, moved his family from Auckland to the small town of Leigh, 50 miles to the north. There, when he was 10, he built his own boat, a 10'6" Flying Ant. "Growing up in New Zealand, you learn to do all sorts of practical things unless you come from a very rich family," he said.

Farr also built 11-foot Moths for pocket money; a distinguishing feature of Farr's Moths was their minimal weight. In a nation where yachting is Everyman's sport, lighter boats use fewer materials and are thus cheaper to build and own. They are also, as Farr and other

Kiwis learned early on, faster. When Farr began work as a yacht designer he became known for his swift offshore boats, and his years of experience in designing light-displacement vessels helped make him a success.

Farr departed New Zealand in 1981. He opened a yacht-design office in Annapolis with fellow Kiwi Russell Bowler, an expert in construction. The first major boat Farr designed in America was *Ceramco*, a long, light boat for the Whitbread Round the World Race. *Ceramco* was sailed by New Zealander Peter Blake. The boat was dismasted on the first leg, from Plymouth, England, to Cape Town, but Blake sailed 4000 miles to South Africa under jury rig. In one day on the passage he logged 240 miles without a true mast. While *Ceramco* didn't win the race, she won two legs.

For the next Whitbread Farr designed three maxis, including race-winner *UBS Switzerland*. In the 1989-90 Whitbread his maxi *Steinlager 2* finished first with Peter Blake at the helm. Blake, who has competed in this race all four times it has been sailed, was the operations manager for Michael Fay's challenge, and Steinlager, the brewery which sponsored Blake in the 1989-90 Whitbread, also became a sponsor of the New Zealand America's Cup effort, along with Toyota and the New Zealand Apple & Pear Marketing Board.

Of the four boats Farr designed for the 1992 Cup, the controversial fourth boat, with its almost plumb bow, lack of side decks, fixed bowsprit — which created such a to-do — and radical forked keel, which only the New Zealanders seemed able to make work, was chosen to represent New Zealand's Mercury Bay Boating Club. *New Zealand* was long on the water and light — reportedly 3000 pounds lighter than the other challengers' boats — and carried less sail. She was more dinghy than maxi — a typical Farr boat, unique among the challengers.

Rod Davis, an American living in New Zealand, was *New Zealand*'s skipper. Davis, age 36, had won an Olympic gold medal in the Soling class, three Congressional Cups — the only man to win that competition three times — and seven world championships.

Davis started sailing in the America's Cup in 1977 as the foredeck man on Lowell North's *Enterprise*. He sailed as mainsheet trimmer in the 1983 America's Cup on *Defender*, with Blackaller and Cayard, and skippered *Eagle* in 1986. He also coached the Kiwis in the "David-and-Goliath" challenge of 1988; although who was David and who was Goliath depends on your perspective.

Davis is the son of Whit Davis, former commander of the submarine *Razorback*; his mother's father was an admiral. He was born in Key West, Florida, and attended high school in Coronado, across the bay from San Diego. He studied accounting but dropped out of college and went to work at North Sails in Seal Beach. After a week there, he asked for time off to sail in the Congressional Cup. He took to match-racing wholeheartedly, and is now ranked among the top five competitors in the world.

At the Citizen Watch Match Racing Series in Auckland, Davis met Liz Schnackenberg, sister of Tom Schnackenberg, a distinguished sail designer for North Sails in New Zealand. Rod and Liz were married, and after 1988 Davis moved to New Zealand, where he lives with his wife and two children.

Peter Blake was operations manager for the New Zealand challenge. Blake has sailed in the Whitbread Round the World Race four times; he won it in 1990 with Steinlager 2.

Above and on the following spread are three of the four New Zealand boats, photographed by Bob Grieser. Opposite is Sir Michael Fay, surrounded by Maoris, the aboriginal people of New Zealand, at a sunrise ceremony at the San Diego Yacht Club.

Rod Davis, an American who lives in New Zealand, skippered the New Zealand boat.

NIPPON CHALLENGE ● JAPAN

When the Nippon Challenge began its quest for the America's Cup, it ran want ads in Japanese newspapers soliciting crew. The ads said "No sailing experience necessary." One prospective crewmember thought he was trying out for a golf tournament. "Not too many in Japan knew what the America's Cup was about," said Tatsumitsu Yamasaki, chairman of the Nippon Challenge. "Everything had to be started from scratch."

Yamasaki is president of S&B Shokuhin Company, a major supplier of sauces and spices to Japan and the world. He is also a yachtsman who has competed in the Admiral's Cup in England and the Kenwood Cup in Hawaii, and is a director of the Nippon Ocean Racing Club, for whom this America's Cup entry sailed. "As a yachtsman it has been my dream to challenge for this prestigious Cup."

In Japan, the dividing line between business and pleasure is, as the world knows, virtually nonexistent. Business *is* the pleasure, so rallying corporate Japan for an America's Cup effort was no easy matter in the beginning, according to Yamasaki.

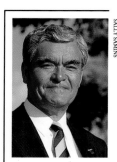

Above is Kaoru Ogimi, vice commodore of the Nippon Ocean Racing Club, which sponsored Nippon. Chris Dickson, left, was skipper.

"When I told them my true intention was to give future generations hopes and dreams on a world scale, then they wanted to help. Japan is often viewed as being business-oriented. This puts our image in a different light."

The America's Cup is, however, a competition ideally suited to the Japanese: The event is technology-driven, and it emphasizes hard work and teamwork. To the Japanese, these requirements are already a cultural ethos.

The syndicate's operating budget of six billion yen, or $40 million, matched the budgets of the best-heeled syndicates in San Diego, including America[3] and Il Moro. The money came from 30 corporate sponsors, including Mazda, Japan Airlines, Mitsubishi, and Yamaha — who built the three Japanese boats, all named *Nippon*. It also came from 38 suppliers and 6800 private individuals.

If the crew came from the want ads, the skipper was headline material — at least in the Auckland papers. The syndicate hired 29-year-old New Zealander Chris Dickson to skipper its boat. Dickson is the top match-racing skipper in the world, although he is perhaps best known as the skipper of *Kiwi Magic*, which sailed so impressively in Australia in 1987.

Dickson's father, Roy, was a noted offshore racer. On his way to regattas, he would drop Chris and his three brothers off at a lake near Auckland. The Dicksons had dinghies there, and the boys played on them for 11 hours a day. At the day's end Roy Dickson would pick up his sons and answer any questions they had.

Dickson's first victory on the international stage was the IYRU World Youth Sailing Championship, in Perth. He won that event two more times, and twice won the Citizen Watch Match Racing Series. He entered the America's Cup arena in 1984 in the 12-Meter Worlds in Sardinia, when he was 22. Using *Enterprise*, a tired 12-Meter that Lowell North had sailed with little success in 1977, Dickson beat Dennis Conner, then a two-time winner and one-time loser of the America's Cup, and John Kolius, whom the

The Japanese built three IACC boats. The first was a generic design by Bruce Farr. The other two were shaped by Ichiro Yokoyama, Kennosuke Hayashi, and Akira Kubota.

On the first day of the finals of the 1991 International America's Cup Class World Championship, the Japanese dropped their carbon-fiber mast over the side. Dickson described that moment as the nadir. Things would improve.

SALLY SAMINS

Aboard Nippon *the language in the cockpit was English; sail trimmers knew enough English — or at least "sailing English" — to translate commands forward in Japanese.*

CARLO BORLENGHI

Whether lowering a spinnaker, as seen above, or raising a mainsail, as seen opposite, the Japanese, newcomers to this event, showed the America's Cup world they had arrived.

New York Yacht Club had anointed as its standard-bearer for Perth. After beating the lions of the America's Cup in that event, Dickson began to think that a conquest of the Cup might just be possible. Not easy, but possible.

Something happened between Dickson and Michael Fay after the 1987 America's Cup. Whatever the cause, Dickson has not sailed for Fay since. Dickson is considered gifted but temperamental; a kind of John McEnroe of match-racing. The Auckland *Star*, for example, headlined a story "Dickson — Super Brat." On the water or on the stage before the media, Dickson seems unflappable and wholly unimpressed by his elders. There is a steeliness to his eyes that could immobolize a snake.

The Japanese signed Dickson for the 1992 event, and Dickson brought along other Kiwis as well, including Olympic bronze medalist John Cutler as tactician; Erle Williams, who had been Dickson's bowman in the 1987 Cup, as navigator; and Mike Spanhake as a sailtrimmer.

The sailing captain and mainsail trimmer aboard *Nippon* was Makoto Namba, a successful Japanese small-boat sailor in such classes as 470 and J/24. In 1990 Namba was ranked tenth in the World Match Racing Conference. The rest of the boat was more than ably manned by the Japanese (most of them culled from responses to those ads), who had trained aboard two fiberglass 12-Meters bought from Michael Fay and a generic IACC design from Kiwi designer Bruce Farr.

Japan, sailing the Farr IACC boat, didn't qualify for the finals of the 1991 IACC World Championship until Dennis Conner opted to protect his sails and his boat by not sailing in the final match-racing segment. On the first day of the finals, *Nippon*'s 110-foot carbon-fiber mast crumpled before a phalanx of media cameras. That moment Dickson describes as the low point.

Japan's second and third boats were designed by a team headed by Ichiro Yokoyama, and including Kennosuke Hayashi and Akira Kubota. The crew jelled in the first round in January, going 6-1 to tie the New Zealand challenge. The Japanese won two races by capitalizing on crew mistakes of the Italians, who sailed to a wrong mark, and the French, who wrapped a spinnaker around the keel. In the second round, the Japanese were 5-2.

In the third round, Peter Blake, operations manager for Sir Michael Fay's New Zealand syndicate, called Dickson a "mercenary and a soldier of fortune." He advised Dickson not to return home to New Zealand. Later Blake apologized. However, Dickson and his Japanese crew beat the Kiwis a couple of days later on March 14 by 1:02. In this round, the Japanese were unbeaten and assumed the series lead. Said crewmember Namba through an interpreter: "Chris has been with us such a long time ... He has eaten the same rice balls. Sailed with us in snow and rain ... He is one of us."

For a team that had started from scratch, the Japanese performance in the 1992 America's Cup was remarkable.

CHALLENGE AUSTRALIA  AUSTRALIA

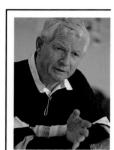

Alan Bond, whose *Australia II* won the Cup in 1983, saw his fortunes change. In 1991 he had to tell some of his creditors at the Tricontinental Corporation in Melbourne that he had only one asset left: a gold watch. They demanded it, but Bond refused to take it off his wrist. According to the Wall Street *Journal*, Bond owed bankers billions. Gone were his breweries, the telephone company in Chile, his yachts, and his van Gogh painting, "Irises," for which he had paid $53.9 million in 1987.

It was the Bond of happier times, however, who inspired countryman Syd Fischer to join the fray. "I saw Bond doing pretty well, and we'd been beating him for about 20 years in ocean racing," said Fischer, "and I thought, if it's that easy, I might as well have a go at it." For 1992 Fischer was head of Challenge Australia, but he is quick to point out that he's not like Bond. "No, I'm not a high-flyer. I try to keep my feet on the ground."

Challenge Australia *was designed by Peter van Oossanen for Syd Fischer.*

A builder from Sydney, Fischer, now 65, has been one of the forces in Australian yachting. The America's Cup, however, has never been easy for Fischer. While *Australia II*, designed by the late Ben Lexcen, was winning the America's Cup in 1983, Fischer's *Advance*, skippered by Iain Murray, was awful. Funded by Fischer, she won but two races all summer. The crew called her a dog and painted a black nose on her bow. When she won a rare race, the shoreside crew pitched dog biscuits at her.

In the 1986-87 Cup, Fischer's boat *Steak 'n Kidney* (Cockney rhyming slang for "Sydney") won four races and lost 27 — although with a new keel she was a vastly improved boat at the end.

Challenge Australia was, like most of Fischer's previous campaigns, primarily self-funded. As such, it was a low-budget operation, at least in comparison to many of his rivals. It was also a one-boat campaign.

Syd Fischer, above, head of the Challenge Australia syndicate, enjoyed more success in ocean racing than in the America's Cup. He won the One Ton Worlds, was the top scorer in the 1971 Admiral's Cup, and has twice won the Sydney-Hobart Race.

Fischer chose Dr. Peter van Oossanen to design *Challenge Australia*. Van Oossanen had helped Lexcen in the design of the winged keel on *Australia II*, and, as a resident of Holland, had been a target of the New York Yacht Club in their attempt to disqualify *Australia II* before the 1983 America's Cup match.

The IACC boat van Oossanen drew for Fischer had a very large bulb under a movable fin keel. The bulb stayed in position but the keel could be canted, changing its angle of attack to the water. It was, says Fischer, supposed to stop the boat from sliding sideways, but it stopped the boat in its tracks. The boat was skippered first by Phil Thompson, who skippered Fischer's *Steak 'n Kidney* in 1986, and later by Hugh Treharne, who skippered *Austalia IV* that same year.

For ten years Syd Fischer has been Everyman at the America's Cup, but he now thinks the common touch doesn't work anymore. The 1992 Cup would be his last, he said. "I don't think I could do another one; I'm too old. It knocks you around too much."

Challenge Australia *was skippered first by Phil Thompson, who steered Fischer's* Steak 'n Kidney *in 1986, and then by Hugh Treharne. Challenge Australia departed after the third round with a record of 1-20.*

Peter van Oossanen designed Challenge Australia. *In 1983 the New York Yacht Club tried to prove that it had been van Oossanen, of Holland, not Ben Lexcen, who designed* Australia II.

SWEDISH AMERICA'S CUP CHALLENGE  SWEDEN

It's been 12 years since Sweden fielded an America's Cup entry. In 1977 and 1980, Sweden's Pelle Petterson skippered *Sverige*, a 12-Meter he designed, in Newport. This was before 12-Meters sprouted wings and long before 12-Meters were obsolete.

For 1992, the next generation of Swedes was back with *Tre Kronor*, an IACC boat skippered by Gunnar Krantz. Krantz, age 36, was raised in Stockholm. He was a watch captain on *The Card* in the 1989-90 Whitbread Round the World Race. The boat, from Sweden, finished fifth.

Four designers — Peter Norlin, Lars Bergstrom, Hakan Sodergren, and Dr. Sven-Olof Ridder — shaped Tre Kronor. *The name means "three crowns," which is the traditional symbol of Swedish battle flags.*

The two enemies of an America's Cup campaign are a lack of time and a lack of money. The Swedish America's Cup Challenge (SACC) suffered from a crippling lack of both. While others flew first-class or at least economy, for the Swedes it was a rocky bus ride. It was, however, promising in the beginning. After the 1987 America's Cup, the Swedes, headed by Tomas Wallin, purchased the 12-Meter *South Australia*, expecting that the next match would be in 12-Meters. In time, Wallin gathered 24 sponsors. Then, with the 1988 monohull versus catamaran match, interest in the America's Cup waned in Sweden as it had in France. Wallin's sponsors lost interest, a recession hit Sweden, and the Cup class was changed from 12-Meter yachts to a much more expensive boat.

Gunnar Krantz was skipper of Tre Kronor. *He has sailed on such notable boats as* Carat, Midnight Sun, *and* The Card. The Card *finished fifth in the Whitbread Round the World Race.*

The Swedes showed they were competitive — at least in 12-Meters — by finishing third in the 1988 12-Meter Worlds in Lulea, Sweden, with their renamed *New Sweden*. The regatta featured most of the name-brand America's Cup talent, including Dennis Conner and Iain Murray. *New Sweden* was skippered by Krantz, who also acted as tactician, and steered by Olle Johansson, a two-time Olympian in the 470 class. That division of labor continued on *Tre Kronor* in the 1992 Cup.

Tre Kronor was designed by Peter Norlin, Lars Bergstrom, Hakan Sodergren, and Dr. Sven-Olof Ridder, and built by Killian Bushe. Primary sponsors included SAAB Automobile, Spendrups, TV3, Nobelpharma, Lufthansa, Polyprodukter AB, Stenungsbaden Yacht Club, and the Hyatt Islandia. The Hyatt Islandia, on Mission Bay, housed the crew and provided space for the boat.

Tre Kronor's first day of sailing in San Diego was January 19, 1992, five days before the Louis Vuitton Cup began. "The lack of time and money before we started sailing made it terribly hard," allowed Krantz. "We had three days on the water before the first race. That's no way to start an America's Cup."

If relatively unsuccessful on the water, the Swedes were enormously popular on land. Their compound was completely open, and visitors were welcome. Even the keel and rudder of the boat were left completely unshrouded — there for the world to see. Asked about this openness, Krantz said, "Actually, we couldn't afford a shroud. We bought a headsail instead."

Krantz described this America's Cup run as "record-setting." As he said, "We arrived late and left early." The Swedes finished with a 3-18 record.

The Swedish compound was open and their boat, including the keel, was visible. Asked about the lack of security, Krantz said, "Actually, we couldn't afford a shroud. We bought a headsail instead."

DESAFIO ESPAÑA COPA AMERICA SPAIN

It was a propitious time for Spain to make its debut at the America's Cup in San Diego, 500 years after Columbus, sailing under the flag of Spain, "discovered" America — actually San Salvador. Spain sailed in the 1992 America's Cup with the appropriately named *España 92-Quinto Centenario*, commemorating Columbus's voyage.

Virtually everyone involved in the America's Cup saw the 1988 match as a turning point in this competition, but few had good things to say about it. For Spain, however, 1988 was positive. It delayed the competition until 1992; thus, it coincided with Columbus's anniversary. "Our original plan was to watch this America's Cup and then try to do the next one," said Pedro Campos, skipper of *España 92-Quinto Centenario*. "However, we had great success raising money because of this anniversary. In fact, our first encouragement came from the Spanish government. If it wasn't for the timing, I doubt we'd have been here."

For the Spanish, a change in class was a positive thing, too. "With a new class, we knew Spain was no farther behind than anyone else," Campos said.

Spain has a proud history in sailing. King Juan Carlos sailed in the 1972 Olympics in the Dragon class, and presently campaigns a One-Tonner, *Bribon*. The country has won seven medals in Olympic sailing, including Gold medals in the Finn class in 1988, the 470 class in 1984, and the Flying Dutchman class in 1980. Antonio Gorostegui, for example, the tactician on *España 92*, won an Olympic silver medal in the 470 class. He is also a two-time world champion in the Star class and a four-time world champion in the 470 class. Pedro Campos, the skipper of *España 92*, won two Three-Quarter Ton World Championships in 1990 and 1991. Campos, who is 36 years old, is also a world champion in the Vaurien Class — a popular dinghy in Europe. He runs Diamond Sails in Spain.

Spain fielded a two-boat program, which sailed for Monte Real Club de Yates de Bayona. The designers of the second boat — the one that sailed in the competition — were Iñigo Echenique, Joaquín González Devesa, Manuel Ruiz Elvira, and Ronaldo Campos. Diego Colón, a naval architect and a direct descendent of Columbus, was the project's technical coordinator.

Major sponsors included Sociedad Estatal Quinto Centenario, the authority set up by the government to run the Columbus Celebration; Astilleros Españoles, which built the boat; Construcciones Aeronáuticas, which worked on the design and construction of the mast and keel; Software AG España, which worked on the velocity-prediction program used to design the boat and supplied the computers; and Radio Television Española, Turespaña, La Casera, Puleva, and Iberia.

Pedro Campos skippered España 92-Quinto Centenario, *seen at left. He is a two-time winner of the Three-Quarter Ton World Championships and a world champion in the Vaurien Class.*

It was an auspicious debut for the Spanish, who finished fifth out of eight challengers in the 1992 America's Cup. Two boats were built; the second one, España 92-Quinto Centenario, *sailed in San Diego.*

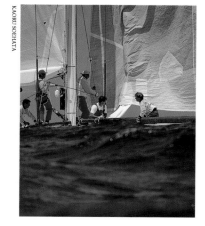

The Spanish crew hoists a spinnaker in the trials. At the end of the third round, when the challenger field was reduced by half, the Spanish departed the scene with a grand gesture: They flew a spinnaker saying, "We love America: 1492–1992." The spinnaker was signed by the entire team. The feelings were mutual.

CHAPTER FOUR

THE HOSTS

San Diego & the San Diego Yacht Club

IN 1988, SAN DIEGO BECAME ONLY the fourth city to host the America's Cup competition. Nevertheless, the 27-inch, 134-ounce silver trophy, cast in 1851, has been most fortunate in terms of racing venues: New York, Newport, Perth, and San Diego. Each place has put its stamp on the America's Cup, and the America's Cup has, in turn, put its stamp on each place.

San Diego, with its 1,094,500 residents, is the second largest city in California and the sixth largest city in America. It has, most apparently, abundant seaside charms and practically perfect weather.

The bay and the climate have long been the focus of San Diegans. The boot-shaped bay is 14 miles long and encompasses 23 square miles of land and sea. San Diego's year-round temperature averages a sublime 70 degrees. That isn't 110 in the summer and 30 in the winter — it's 70 degrees year-round.

Modern San Diego is a sprawling, busy, ever-interesting city. The bay is visually accessible and approachable

The San Diego County
Administration Center, on Pacific
Highway. The statue, done by
Donal Hord in 1939, is entitled
"Guardian of Water."

The popular Killer Whale Show at
Sea World in Mission Bay.
Opposite is the famous Hotel del
Coronado, across the bay from San
Diego. On the following spread is a
view of San Diego from Point
Loma, taken by Kaoru Soehata.
The building in the foreground
with the cupola is the San Diego
Yacht Club; behind it is manmade
Shelter Island. Downtown San
Diego lies across the bay.

the railroad tracks.

The year after the railroad arrived, the population of San Diego swelled from
6204 residents to 24,000. During the boom, which ran from 1885 to 1888, trains and
ships arriving in San Diego were met by representatives from the Chamber of
Commerce, as well as from various real-estate offices. Prospective buyers were piled
into wagons and taken to view property, often accompanied by marching bands. In
weeks, the value of property doubled. It was heady stuff.

The year 1885 was a good one for San Diego. In addition to the arrival of the
railroad, a partnership composed of Hampton L. Story, of Cambridge, Massachusetts,
and Elisha S. Babcock Jr., of Evansville, Indiana, purchased the rights to the Coronado
Peninsula for $110,000. They hoped to build a resort hotel and develop the land.
In those days, Coronado was two "islands," North and South Island, separated by a
marshy bight. The marsh would eventually be filled by the Navy, which today runs the
U. S. Naval Air Station on North Island. South Island is actually a peninsula,
connected to the mainland by the Silver Strand and now, of course, by the elegantly
curved and towering 2.2-mile Coronado Bay Bridge, completed in 1969. While
technically a peninsula, Coronado, then and now, has the unmistakable feel of an island
— a place that runs at a very different pace from hustling and broad-shouldered San
Diego.

On March 19, 1887, ground was broken for the Hotel del Coronado, designed by
brothers James and Merritt Reid, who would later design such famous San Francisco
landmarks as the Fairmont Hotel and Cliff House. When the Victorian-style hotel, with
its spectacular view of the Pacific, opened in 1888, the San Diego *Union* trumpeted, "A
Hotel That is Surpassed by None in the World." The hotel was designated a National
Historic Landmark in 1977.

Sixty-five movies have used the Hotel del Coronado as a backdrop; most notably
"Some Like It Hot," starring Marilyn Monroe and Jack Lemmon. Twelve American
presidents have stayed there, as well as such luminaries as Thomas A. Edison, who
decorated a Christmas tree at the hotel with electric lights in 1904 (the first time this
was ever done).

The Prince of Wales was entertained at a lavish ball at the Hotel del Coronado in
1920. It could well have been at the hotel that the future King met Mrs. Wallis Warfield
Simpson, who was then married to the commanding officer of the U. S. Naval Air
Station on North Island. As King Edward VIII, he would abdicate the British throne to
marry "the woman I love" in 1936.

In 1887, John D. Spreckels, son of Claus, the "Sugar King" of Hawaii and San
Francisco, arrived in San Diego on his 87-foot schooner *Lurline*. Like Horton,
Spreckels liked what he saw; and like Horton, he left a huge imprint on the town.

Spreckels ended up purchasing much of the development on Coronado, including
the Hotel del Coronado. He built in San Diego in the area bounded by Broadway and
Fifth Street. He owned two newspapers, one of which was the San Diego *Union*, still
published today as a Copley paper. It was also Spreckels, described as "San Diego's
foremost citizen," who brought what San Diegans wanted so badly: a direct railroad
connection to the East, through the San Diego & Arizona Railway. The line went from
San Diego's harbor, east to the Imperial Valley, and to the main line of the Southern

Pacific in Arizona.

Spreckels also owned the San Diego Electric Railway Company. It was this transportation network, which he rebuilt and electrified, that accounted for the development of such San Diego neighborhoods as La Jolla, Ocean Beach, Pacific Beach, and University Heights.

To appeal to riders, it was important that the streetcar lines have an attraction at their terminus. Spreckels built an amusement park at Mission Beach, which included a roller-coaster 75 feet high. The amusement park and a refurbished roller-coaster are still there. In 1949, the area was further developed into Mission Bay Park. Built on what used to be known as False Bay, where the San Diego River also emptied from time to time, this project is today a jewel of an aquatic park, which spans 4600 acres. On a peak-season weekend, the park is visited by 100,000 people. This area is also the home of Sea World, which rivals the famous San Diego Zoo as the major tourist attraction of the city.

Above is the Gaslamp Quarter in downtown San Diego, which features the Victorian-style architecture popularized by Alonzo Erastus Horton. Opposite is Horton Plaza, an exuberant, multi-tiered shopping center punctuated by more than a dozen architectural styles. The plaza was built in 1985 as an urban-renewal project.

Perhaps because it is situated in an isolated corner of the country, San Diego has never been shy about advertising its considerable charms to the world. Indeed "boosterism" is endemic and has been almost since the beginning. For example, in 1892, the San Diego *Sun* newspaper suggested a "Cabrillo Celebration," to commemorate Cabrillo's 1542 voyage. Promotional activities included bombs — loaded with promotional literature about the festival — that were exploded above bathers at Redondo Beach, near Los Angeles.

In 1915-16 San Diego hosted the Panama California Exposition. This event coincided with the opening of the Panama Canal. It was expected that San Diego would be a port of call for commercial vessels passing into and out of the canal. This never happened, however, as such ships ended up bypassing San Diego for the manmade harbor in the Los Angeles area.

It was Colonel D. C. Collier who took charge of the Panama California Exposition and designated Balboa Park as the site. The 1400-acre site Alonzo Horton had helped to select in 1867 was first called "City Park" but eventually Balboa Park. Collier also chose what was called the "Spanish-Colonial" or "neo-Spanish" style of architecture for the buildings that would house the exhibits. This architectural style, first brought to San Diego by Father Serra, remains important here to this day.

Above is the El Cid statue at Balboa Park. Balboa Park is the cultural heart of San Diego.

The 1915-16 Exposition and a similar one in 1935-36, called the California Pacific International Exposition, left an indelible mark on Balboa Park. Today, the elegant buildings there, many of which can be traced to these exhibitions, house the Old Globe Theater, the Museum of Man, the Aerospace Museum, the Natural History Museum, the Botanical Garden, and the Spreckels Organ Pavilion. The park is also home to the San Diego Zoo.

Much of the park's beauty today can be traced to Kate Sessions, who planted seeds from Asia, Australia, Spain, South American, New England, and California. This resulted in the very rare Torrey pines, Monterey cypress, pepper trees, cork oaks, and, of course, eucalyptus trees that characterize the area. Balboa Park is to San Diego what Central Park is to New York City or Golden Gate Park is to San Francisco: The city would be a far different place without it.

The America's Cup reached out to the San Diego community with such programs

CARLO BORLENGHI

The America's Cup Museum featured Rolly Tasker's models of defenders and challengers since 1851, historic photographs from Mystic Seaport's Rosenfeld Collection, and interactive computer programs from Hewlett-Packard and PACT. On the following spread is a Kirk Schlea photograph of the Jack Murphy Stadium.

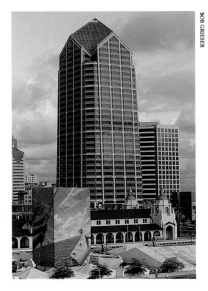

BOB GRIESER

In the foreground is the America's Cup International Centre. The tall building is the newly constructed America Plaza building, built by Shimizu, which housed the AT&T America's Cup Media Center. On the opposite page is a detail of "Reaching for Victory," a 21,500 square-foot painting by Catherine Feff, commissioned by AT&T.

as the America's Cup Museum, the America's Cup International Centre, and the America's Cup Youth Education Program.

The America's Cup Museum was a one-year exhibit of America's Cup memorabilia — the likes of which have never been assembled before. In its 5000 square feet, the museum featured America's Cup mementos — including the rudder of the yacht *America*; Rolly Tasker's models of all the defenders and challengers since 1851; and historic photographs from Mystic Seaport's famed Rosenfeld Collection. Also on site were interactive computer programs from Hewlett-Packard and the Partnership for America's Cup Technology (PACT), the design consortium for defenders. The museum also displayed a scoreboard from Challenger of Record Sponsor, Louis Vuitton, showing race scores for both challengers and defenders.

The America's Cup International Centre, adjacent to the Santa Fe train depot, was sponsored by American Telephone & Telegraph (AT&T). It served as the official gathering place for America's Cup followers and residents. It was, in essence, an America's Cup theme park. The Centre, on space donated by the Catellus Corporation, offered food indigenous to the competing nations, interactive educational displays (including a motion-based simulator), a T.G.I. Friday's restaurant, and entertainment on Thursdays, Fridays, and Saturdays. Its centerpiece was a cube-shaped 21,500 square-foot painting, "Reaching for Victory," by Catherine Feff, of France. Also on display there was *Il Moro di Venezia*, the first Italian International America's Cup Class boat.

The America's Cup Youth Education Program brought the America's Cup into local classrooms. Sponsored by the San Diego Unified Port District, its theme was "Believe, Achieve & Succeed." The program, developed and implemented by Palmer, Sharrit & Co., tied the America's Cup to academic subjects such as foreign languages, social studies, history, geography, math, and fine arts with curriculums aimed at every grade level. It involved 20,000 teachers and 400,000 students in San Diego.

Newport, Rhode Island — the long-time home of the America's Cup — is relentlessly "yachty" — almost a one-note samba. Perth, where they raced for the Cup in 1986-87, occupies an exotic corner of the earth, with wind, kangaroos, and "put-another-shrimp-on-the-barbie" cordiality. Both places, essentially, are busy but insular towns. San Diego, by contrast, is a large, mature city with a host of competing attractions. It was to this place that the America's Cup world came in 1988 and again in 1992. The America's Cup had not been contested in a major metropolitan area since the XIV Defense in 1920 — the last defense in New York.

THE SAN DIEGO YACHT CLUB

On June 8, 1886, a year after the Santa Fe Railroad had helped quadruple the population of San Diego, 55 people gathered in Horton's Hall to form the San Diego Rowing Club. As an afterthought, says Charles La Dow in his book on the San Diego Yacht Club, entitled *The Ships, the House, and the Men*, they started a yacht club, too. This became the San Diego Yacht Club (SDYC), which would, of course, become the trustee of the America's Cup almost 102 years later.

The first meeting of the San Diego Yacht Club was held on Ballast Point, in the living quarters of the lighthouse on Point Loma. The SDYC continued meeting in these

quarters until 1898 when the building was expropriated for the Spanish-American War. The club became homeless and, indeed, rudderless.

In 1902, the commodore of the San Diego Yacht Club was Lucien A. Blochman, a banker and financier. He was one of the very few members to own a boat, in this case a large motor-yacht, *Haidee*. Dissatisfied with the homeless club and the lack of boats, Blochman left to found the Corinthian Yacht Club of San Diego.

The next year, Commodore Blochman wrote a letter to Sir Thomas Lipton asking if the tea magnate would lend his name to a local trophy. Lipton, then involved in his third America's Cup challenge with *Shamrock III*, wrote back saying he wasn't sure whether the club wanted merely his name or a trophy, but that he would be happy to provide either. The Corinthians were overjoyed and asked for a trophy. Sir Thomas sent them a 32-inch silver trophy, the Lipton Cup — one of several Lipton Cups that he donated to various sporting events.

In 1904, several members of the San Diego Yacht Club decided to challenge the Corinthians for the Lipton Cup. They chartered the 47-foot *Detroit* from the Great Lakes, for $25, brought her to San Diego, and easily triumphed over four other yachts in two races in Coronado Roads.

Detroit was sold to a South Coast Yacht Club syndicate, and with the boat went the Lipton Cup to the club's home in San Pedro, near Los Angeles. The result was a Southern California inter-club competition that survives to this day. The SDYC has won the Lipton Cup more than any other Southern California club; winning skippers include Dennis Conner, Lowell North, and Malin Burnham, all of whom have played leading roles in the America's Cup.

In 1905, the SDYC, temporarily situated on donated land on La Playa, had a deficit of $198.34. The Corinthian Yacht Club, which was considered a "more lively place," had a more lively deficit of $790. So the two clubs merged. They retained the San Diego Yacht Club name but took the Corinthian burgee, designed by Commodore Blochman, for their symbol. A big impetus for keeping the Corinthian burgee was, doubtless, that its likeness appeared on the Lipton Cup. This is the symbol of the SDYC today. The club took over the quarters of the Corinthian Yacht Club on D Street —

Joe Jessop Sr. impressed Sir Thomas Lipton with his boatbuilding skills in 1913. In 1929, he was commodore of the San Diego Yacht Club. Jessop also brought the first Star to San Diego.

what is now Broadway. The club also arranged for the Deed of Gift governing the Lipton Cup to be transferred from the Corinthian to the San Diego Yacht Club.

SDYC member Alonzo Jessop, whose family owned jewelry stores in downtown San Diego, handled the correspondence with Sir Thomas Lipton. The two became friends. Lipton, at Jessop's urgings, came to San Diego. Jessop took Lipton out to see the harbor, which Lipton pronounced "the most beautiful harbor in the world."

Joseph E. Jessop Sr., commodore of the SDYC in 1929, is now 93. He was 15 when Lipton paid his visit and remembers his brother Alonzo bringing Lipton out to the family house on Coronado for supper. "I had built a boat; an awful-looking boat out of wooden packing crates that brought merchandise to the jewelry stores," Jessop recalled. "Sir Thomas came to dinner and was such a genial guy, you couldn't help but love him. During the meal, he learned

In 1905, the San Diego Yacht Club merged with the Corinthian Yacht Club and took over the latter's building on D Street — or Broadway. Opposite is the Convention Center.

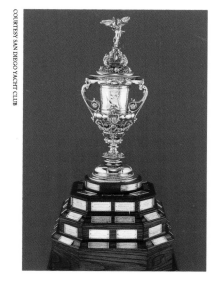

Sir Thomas Lipton, whose Shamrock III *was challenging for the America's Cup in 1903, gave the Corinthian Yacht Club a Lipton Cup that year. The San Diego Yacht Club won the first Lipton Cup match in 1904 and has won it more than any other Southern California yacht club. Winning SDYC skippers include Dennis Conner, Lowell North, and Malin Burnham. Like the Star World Championships, the Lipton Cup has been a link between the America's Cup and SDYC sailors.*

about my boat. After supper, he said, 'Joe, I want to see it.' We wandered out to the backyard. Lipton put his arm around me and said, 'Joe, it looks like a winner to me; I think I should buy it from you.'"

When the Santa Fe Railroad decided to use the area where the SDYC was housed, the clubhouse was abandoned. In 1910 the SDYC purchased the *Silver Gate*, a former ferryboat, from John B. Spreckels, "San Diego's foremost citizen," and had it towed a few blocks north to Hawthorn Street. The *Silver Gate* had most recently been a dancing pavilion at Spreckels's famous Coronado Tent City, a summer campground.

Spreckels was a member of the SDYC and an enthusiastic yachtsman. His *Lurline*, the boat that first brought him to San Diego in 1887, won the Honolulu Race, now the Transpac, in 1906, 1908, and 1912, while sailing under the burgee of the San Diego Yacht Club.

In 1914, when the Embarcadero wished to extend its seawall, the ferryboat clubhouse was towed to Coronado. At this out-of-the-way site and with the effects of the First World War, membership dwindled. The SDYC then moved a total of nine times before arriving at its present site in 1923, on leased Port District land in Point Loma. The current SDYC building opened in 1963.

SDYC's famous Junior Sailing Program was started by Joe Jessop Sr., in 1928. That same year, Jessop finished third in the Star World Championship and brought the first Star-class boat to San Diego. High-level competition in the Star, a 22'8" sloop designed by William Gardner in 1911, would link the sailing careers of several notable SDYC sailors with the America's Cup. For example, Joe Jessop Sr., managed a syndicate that fielded *Columbia*, an unsuccessful defense contender in 1967. In 1974, San Diego boatbuilder and club member Gerry Driscoll, a Star World Champion in 1944, sailed a rebuilt *Intrepid* in a pitched battle against the new Sparkman & Stephens-designed *Courageous*, before the latter boat was selected to defend.

Aboard *Courageous* that year was 32-year-old Dennis Conner, making his America's Cup debut. Conner had won the Star Worlds in 1971 and would win it again in 1977. He would, of course, go on to defend the America's Cup in 1980, lose it in 1983, regain it in Western Australia in 1987, and bring it home to San Diego and defend it in 1988.

Lowell North, the famous sailmaker, skippered *Enterprise* in the 1977 America's Cup. North's helmsman that year was Malin Burnham. In 1944, Burnham, age 15, had crewed for Gerry Driscoll when they won the Star World Championship. The next year Burnham skippered a Star to the World Championship with 15-year-old Lowell North as crew. Burnham ran Dennis Conner's Sail America syndicate for 1986-87 and 1988 and was president and chairman of the America's Cup Organizing Committee (ACOC) for the 1992 event. North won a total of four Star World Championships.

When Dennis Conner brought the America's Cup home to San Diego in February 1987, Joe Jessop Sr. was asked what the America's Cup would mean to the San Diego Yacht Club. "Baby, we've come a long way!" he said.

The Silver Gate *became home of the San Diego Yacht Club in 1910. When she developed dry-rot a few years later and had to be scrapped, the club moved nine times before arriving at its present site in 1923, on leased Port District land in Point Loma.*

COURTESY SAN DIEGO YACHT CLUB

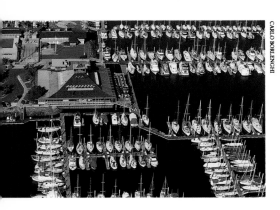

The present building of the San Diego Yacht Club opened in 1963. Today, the SDYC has about 1800 members, 575 slips, two tennis courts, a swimming pool, restaurant, bar, dry-boat storage, and 100 employees. Opposite is Point Loma.

CARLO BORLENGHI

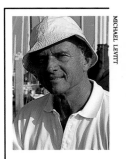

MICHAEL LEVITT

Lowell North, the noted sailmaker, is one of several San Diego Yacht Club members who dominated the Star Class before sailing in the America's Cup.

CHAPTER FIVE

DEFENDERS OF THE FAITH

Defense Trials

FROM DENNIS CONNER'S perspective, David met Goliath in the defense trials. Conner, of course, was David, and Bill Koch was Goliath. However, Koch was no ordinary giant; each time Conner seemed to draw a bead on him, Koch transformed himself into a new and ever more fearsome form.

From Koch's perspective, Conner was the proverbial cat with nine lives. Koch had him all but eliminated in the second round, when *Stars & Stripes* sported her painfully slow tandem keel. However, when Koch allowed Conner to change his keel in the middle of the round, Conner escaped his clutches and won two races that he almost certainly would have lost with the tandem keel. These two victories, seemingly of little import back then, helped Conner carry one bonus point into the semifinals. Without that point, there wouldn't have been a sail-off between *Kanza* and *Stars & Stripes*. Conner won the sail-off, and advanced to the finals.

In the best-of-thirteen finals, Koch, with his super boat

In prestart action during the defense trials, Stars & Stripes, *in the foreground, tacks in front of* America³.

America³, won the first three races. He lost the fourth and then won the fifth, making the score 4-1. Conner then won the next three races to tie the score. Said David Dellenbaugh, tactician and starting helmsman on *America³*, "We kept asking ourselves: What do we have to do to knock this guy down and keep him there?"

ROUND ONE

Round one began on January 14, with Koch's new boat, *Defiant* beating Conner's *Stars & Stripes* by 1:34. It was a gun-to-gun win for the Buddy Melges-skippered *Defiant*. On day two, Koch steered *Jayhawk*, his second boat entered in the trials, and lost to *Stars & Stripes* by 4:10. In the this race, San Diego showed an unexpected fickleness: The race started with the wind at 020 degrees and finished with it at 230 degrees; it varied in strength from 18 knots at the start to seven knots at the finish. Upwind legs ended with spinnakers, downwind legs ended with reaching gennakers. Amazingly, the race committee was able to keep the course aligned to the ever-shifting wind.

Confusion aside, shifty winds and windspeed differences guaranteed passing lanes in which a boat behind could get ahead. While never of this magnitude again, the changing conditions made the racing compelling and allowed Conner, sailing an old and relatively slow boat, to stay more than competitive.

On day three, January 16, Melges in *Defiant* beat Koch in *Jayhawk* by 3:47 in an *America³* intramural match. This pattern characterized the nine races in round one: *Defiant*, which finished first, beat *Stars & Stripes* in their three matches, and beat *Jayhawk* in their three intramurals. *Stars & Stripes*, which finished second, beat *Jayhawk* in their three matches.

ROUND TWO

In round two, Koch's *America³* syndicate took a giant step forward with the launch of its new boat, *America³*. Meanwhile, Conner's *Stars & Stripes* took a giant step backward with its tandem keel — like that on *New Zealand*.

In the first race, on February 8, *America³*, just out of the box, won by a monumental 6:23 over the floundering *Stars & Stripes*. In race two, sailed in a windy 18 knots, Bill Koch steered *Defiant* to victory over *Stars & Stripes* by 4:16. In race three, *Defiant* suffered her first loss, to stable-mate *America³*, by 49 seconds. In race four, on February 11, *America³* beat *Stars & Stripes* by 6:00. That meant that in three races, Conner, the veritable King of the America's Cup, had lost by an average margin of 5:33.

A meeting was held at the *America³* compound to decide whether to allow Conner to make what was termed a "mid-series mode change," which was not permitted under the rules. The vote against letting Conner off the mat was 14-1; however, the one vote for it was cast by Bill Koch. That vote carried the day.

David Dellenbaugh put this grand gesture into perspective two days after *America³* successfully defended the America's Cup: "You have to look back at it now and say it was the right thing to do. It was always our plan to eliminate *Stars & Stripes* as quickly as possible, to guarantee ourselves two boats in the defender finals and a berth in the Cup match. We just missed doing that. I think, in our hearts, it was disappointing for everyone; on the other hand, in our heads, everyone knew it was

On January 14 — the first day of the Defender Elimination Series — Stars & Stripes departs her dock to do battle with Defiant. Defiant, Bill Koch's second boat, would win the inaugural race by 1:34. Opposite is a masthead view of Stars & Stripes. On the next spread is a Sally Samins photo of Stars & Stripes to leeward and ahead of Defiant.

going to be better for us to race Dennis in the finals than to sail against ourselves."

In return for allowing Conner to change keels, Koch was given the right to make a mid-series change to one of his boats at a later date.

A reconfigured *Stars & Stripes* beat *Defiant* the next day by 55 seconds. This was *Stars & Stripes*'s first victory over *Defiant*, and the first loss in 11 races for Melges.

At the end of the round, on February 18, *America³* was in first place — her only loss had been when she crossed the starting line early in a race with her stable-mate, *Defiant*. *Stars & Stripes*, thanks to the mid-series mode change, was in second — after beating *Defiant* a second time — and *Defiant* was in third.

One loss aside, *America³* proved to be a magnificent boat. Most important and most apparent, she was the narrowest boat in San Diego, and this lack of beam made her very effective in light winds and rough seas — the typical San Diego condition. Beyond this, she performed exactly the way Koch's design team had said she would, which gave the syndicate huge and deserved faith in its designers. In later rounds, the syndicate would trust its designers sufficiently to make changes — even radical changes in the midst of playing a winning hand — with no on-the-water testing.

Finally, while Koch's team didn't admit it then, *America³*, despite her narrowness, which results in less inherent stability, showed dazzling and unexpected speed in a breeze. With the boat's heavy-weather performance assured, the design team could focus on further improving her light-air performance.

By comparison, *Stars & Stripes*, as would be seen in the next round, was painted into a very narrow design corner: She was optimized for five to seven knots of wind and smooth seas. In truth, Conner's corner was even narrower than that. His *Stars & Stripes* was generally faster on port tack than starboard. With San Diego's typical northwesterly winds, coupled with the normal westerly swell, the boats headed more directly into the waves on starboard tack. A wider boat like *Stars & Stripes* was a bigger target and suffered more on starboard tack than the very narrow *America³*.

Conner, ever the cat with nine lives, got his optimum conditions — five to seven knots and smooth seas, surprisingly often. He was helped by an El Niño — an abnormally warm offshore current, which seemed to still the winds and calm the seas.

ROUND THREE

Round three started on March 3 with *America³* beating *Stars & Stripes* by 1:11. Nothing surprising there, except that *America³* had the fastest time of any challenger or defender around the 20-mile course, at 2:16:16. *Stars & Stripes* had the second fastest time that day at 2:17:27. *Il Moro* was the only boat to break either of these records; on March 10, in a breeze that built to 18 knots, her time was 2:10:36.

Few in the media were impressed, however. The day after *America³* and *Stars & Stripes* notched these times, the Italian magazine *Mondo Barca* released its media poll. *New Zealand* was ranked first; *Il Moro* was second; *Nippon*, third; *America³* was fourth; and *Stars & Stripes*, fifth. A month later, in the same magazine's poll, the ranking of the American boats was unchanged but *Nippon* moved ahead of *Il Moro*.

What accounted for the personality change in *Stars & Stripes*? The structure needed to support the boat's trick keel had been removed, eliminating 300 pounds. Meanwhile, her traditional "monoplane" keel had sprouted wings and her sails

Above, while waiting for the wind, a Defiant *crewmember catches up on his reading. Opposite,* Defiant *powers upwind. She was untouchable in the first round, going 6-0.* Stars & Stripes *was 3-3 in this round, and* Jayhawk, *also in the* America³ *stable, was 0-6.*

continued to improve.

In race two, in 14 knots of wind, *Stars & Stripes* beat *Defiant* by 2:15, after *Defiant* broke a spinnaker pole. Again Conner notched a new second-fastest time — at 2:16:37. Now Conner had beaten *Defiant*, a boat he couldn't get near in the first round, three straight times.

Then the bottom fell out. In race four, on March 6, *America³* beat *Stars & Stripes* by 5:33. On day five, *Defiant* beat *Stars & Stripes* by 1:19, after Conner struck a 70-foot powerboat during the pre-start maneuvering. Then the top fell off. In race seven on March 10, *Stars & Stripes* was dismasted when a backstay block failed. This was the day *Il Moro* set the course record. Conner's crew worked much of the night to replace the mast, but *Stars & Stripes* lost to *Defiant* the next day by 23 seconds.

Conner was now in last place. However, just when the press was about to write his obituary, as it had been about to do in the second round, Conner finished the series with a start-to-finish win over *America³* by 1:05 in the tenth race on March 13, and a win over *Defiant* the next day by 38 seconds.

The round ended with *America³* in first place, *Stars & Stripes* in second, and *Defiant*, which was about to be replaced by Koch's fourth boat, *Kanza*, in third.

SEMIFINALS

The scoring in the defender series was complex, to say the least. The first-place boat, going into the semifinals, was given two points; the second-place boat, one point; and the third-place boat, no points. Thus, one of Koch's boats was entitled to two points, as garnered by *America³*; the other boat would enter with no points — the legacy of *Defiant*. With an all-Koch final as the team's imperative, Koch opted to give the new boat, *Kanza*, the two points, or the equivalent of two wins, and leave his proven boat, *America³*, with none. *Stars & Stripes* entered the round with one point.

Stars & Stripes beat the new *Kanza* and then *America³* in the first two days of racing in the semifinals. This was *Stars & Stripes*'s second straight win over the seemingly invincible *America³*.

Again *Stars & Stripes* had undergone major modifications: She now sported a new bulb, new wings, new trim tab, and new rudder. The trim tab and rudder had been made shorter front to back and shaped better to decrease drag. The stern of the boat had been rebuilt, saving 100 pounds; 40 pounds of extra weight had been removed from the bow, and the mast had been lightened considerably. The aim in taking weight out of the extremities — stern, bow, and mast — was to decrease pitching.

It was during the second race, on March 31, that Bill Koch took the wheel of *America³* on the first leg. Normally, after Dellenbaugh started the boat, Melges would take the helm for the first three legs, and Koch would steer on the three reaching legs. Koch had a 10-second lead and was on what appeared to be the favored right side of the course. Conner was forced left, and he made some gains there. When Conner came back on port tack, heading for the right side of the course, he passed behind *America³*. *America³*, rather than tacking on *Stars & Stripes*, allowed Conner to go right. Perhaps the brain trust concluded that the pendulum had swung to favor the left side. But there was more wind on the right, as well as a right-hand (clockwise) shift, and by the first mark Conner led by 25 seconds. He went on to a fourth straight victory.

BOB GRIESER

Above is another view of Defiant. *On the opposite page,* Stars & Stripes *was dismasted at the first mark on one of the windiest days of the trials on March 10. Gone were a new $500,000 carbon-fiber mast and a new $50,000 Kevlar mainsail. With her old mast,* Stars & Stripes *lost the next race; it was a close race, however, with a delta of 23 seconds. Then she won the last two races and gave Dennis Conner a new lease on life.*

KIRK SCHLEA

Kanza *was the fourth and final boat built by the* America³ *syndicate. She was designed for heavier winds, something there wasn't much of in the semifinals.* Kanza *lost a sail-off to* Stars & Stripes, *and the latter boat and* America³ *moved on to the finals.*

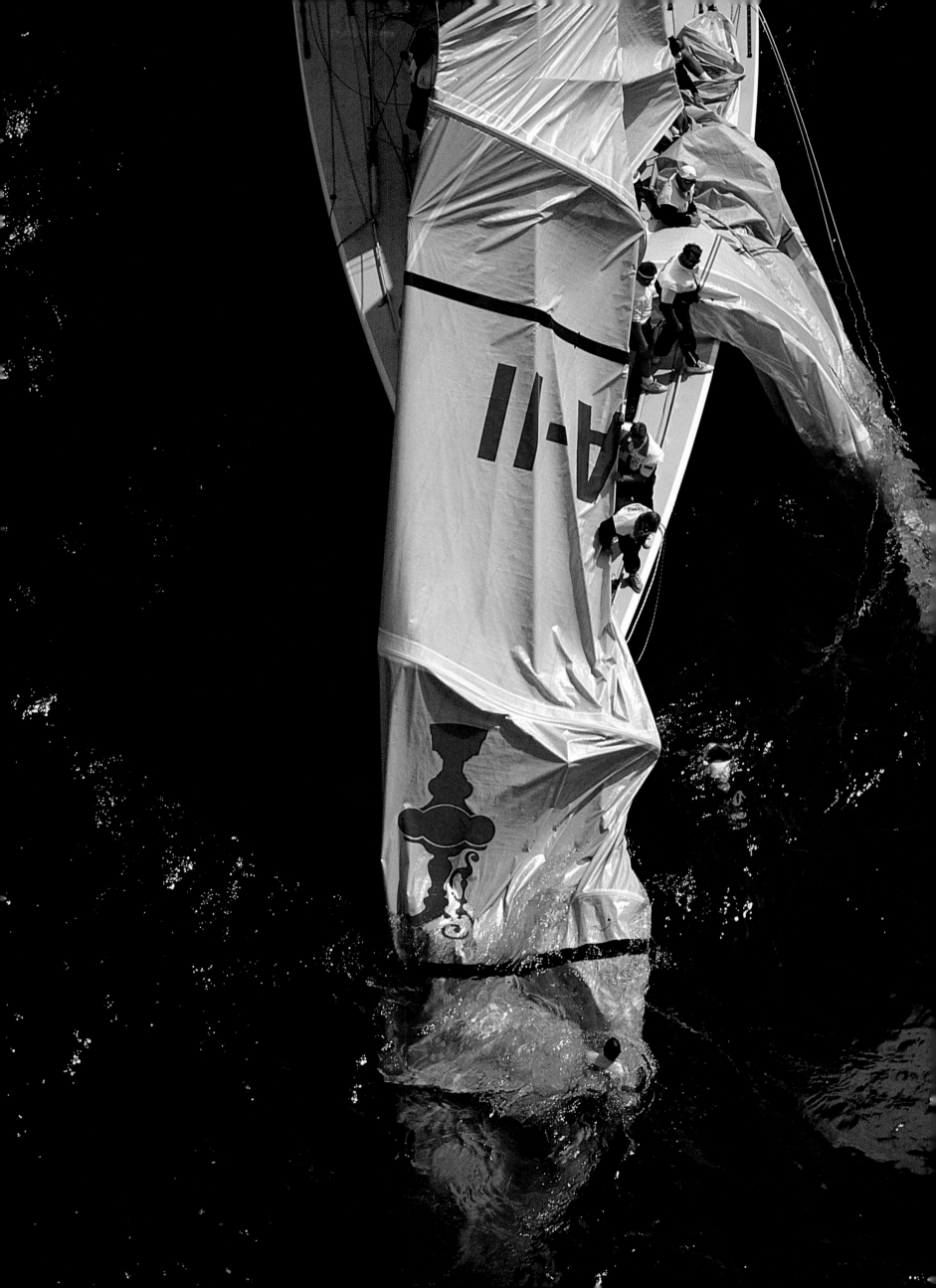

Koch took tremendous heat from the media for taking the wheel that day. In truth, the decision not to cover Conner was the responsibility of the brain trust, the tactician and helmsman. Had the wind swung left, or had there been more velocity on that side, they would have been the toast of the town. But it didn't, and Bill Koch wasn't. *Stars & Stripes* was now alone in first place.

It was even worse in the next race when Koch, steering *America³*, fouled *Kanza* by tacking too close. *America³* was forced to do a penalty turn and lost the race. On April 2, *Kanza* beat *Stars & Stripes* by 42 seconds, in her conditions — the wind built to 14 knots at the finish.

Despite the win, things were getting strange at the America³ compound on Harbor Drive. On April 4, Melges was benched and Kimo Worthington — a new face in the crowd — steered *America³* against *Stars & Stripes*. Before his promotion, Worthington, from Oakland, California, had been an alternate mainsheet trimmer with the syndicate. His America's Cup experience included *Clipper* in 1980 and *Eagle* in 1986. On the third leg, *Stars & Stripes* took the lead and won the race by 1:56.

It was five races into the round, and *America³* — the best boat in San Diego by a nautical mile — had yet to win a race. On April 5 her fortune changed: She beat her stable-mate *Kanza*, after *Kanza*, steered by Bill Koch, broke her spinnaker pole in a jibing duel. If adversity builds character, the America³ team was gaining considerable character at this point in the series.

One of the most interesting and most controversial defender races of the season was sailed on April 7, between *Stars & Stripes* and *Kanza*. *Stars & Stripes* led *Kanza* until the end of leg six by 34 seconds. On the final weather leg, *Kanza* passed *Stars & Stripes* on pure boatspeed in 12 knots of wind. Just before reaching a circle two boatlengths from the mark, *Stars & Stripes* tacked first to port, passing behind *Kanza*. Immediately, *Kanza* tacked over, too, staying between the mark and the competition. As the boats entered the two-boatlength circle on port tack (see the right-hand figure), *Kanza*, as the inside boat, was entitled to room to round the mark, under Rule 42.1 (a).

There is, however, a very small exception to this rule: IYRU Rule 42.3 (a) (ii) reads, "However, when a yacht completes a tack within two of her overall lengths of a mark or obstruction, she shall give room as required by Rule 42.1(a) to a yacht that, by luffing, cannot thereafter avoid establishing a late inside overlap."

Conner, with his typical racecourse brilliance and gunslinger confidence, pushed through that small and arcane opening. He tacked to starboard; then *Kanza* also tacked to round the mark. Now *Stars & Stripes*, as the inside boat, seemed to be entitled to room.

However, even if *Stars & Stripes* was entitled to room at the mark as the inside boat, the outside boat has to be "able" to give room. A question the umpires doubtless asked themselves was whether there was time for *Kanza* to give *Stars & Stripes* room.

A gentle collision occurred between the yachts. After the collision, *Stars & Stripes* bounced into the mark. Both boats flew protest flags. The umpires, who were in a good position to see it, green-flagged the incident between the yachts, which meant that there was no foul, or they couldn't agree who was at fault. They penalized Conner, however, for hitting the mark, requiring him to perform a 270-degree penalty turn before the finish. Conner opted not to do it until the very end. On the run to the finish,

Opposite, Stars & Stripes *rounds a mark ahead of* America³, *USA 23. Above,* America³ *luminaries watch a race. On the left-hand side of the photo are, left to right, Doug Peterson, an* America³ *yacht designer, Vincent Moeyersoms, executive vice president, Harold Cudmore, coach, and Bill Koch, syndicate head and skipper.*

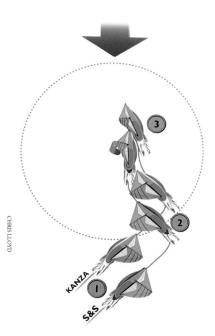

Kanza *enters a circle two boatlengths from the mark in Position 1. As the inside boat, she is entitled to room. However,* Stars & Stripes *tacks to starboard inside the circle, becoming the inside boat with rights (Position 2). This change in right-of-way is countenanced by a small opening under Rule 42.3(a) (ii). A collision occurred at Position 3, and then* Stars & Stripes *bounced into the mark. The umpires green-flagged the collision but penalized* Stars & Stripes *for hitting the mark.*

behind. Conner tacked onto port, fighting to get back to the right of *America³* and toward the middle of the course. *America³* on starboard tack, had the right-of-way, and Conner wanted to cross her. On the approach, Tom Whidden told Conner he wasn't going to make it. "We'll see about that," said Conner. "Watch this!" At the last second, however, Conner kept clear by tacking just to leeward of *America³*.

The next time they came together, Conner went for it. So close was the crossing that Conner had to bear way at the last second to keep the stern of his boat from being hit by the bow of *America³*. Conner was now ahead and in control on the inside of the course. What ensued was a glorious cat-and-mouse game, in which Conner allowed *America³* to sail on starboard tack, ever closer to the left-hand layline and *America³* fought to sail on port tack. Every time *America³* tacked onto port tack, Conner tacked on her wind. When *America³* tacked to starboard, toward the layline, Conner was far more generous, with a loose cover.

There were 20 tacks in the sequence, and *America³* was gaining on the tacks. Finally Conner announced, "He's going to have me at the next crossing."

As *America³* tacked from starboard to port, Conner stayed on port, too. At this point, *America³* was to weather by a boatlength, and behind. However, she was going a knot faster and sailing higher. As *America³* moved to pass *Stars & Stripes* to weather, Conner luffed Melges on *America³* (see top right-hand figure). With the luff, *America³* almost stopped. At that instant, Conner called for sailtrimmer John Sangmeister to ease the headsail. Conner's boat accelerated into the lead and worked itself to weather. Then on the layline and to weather, *Stars & Stripes* hurt *America³* all the way to the mark. Conner's boat rounded ahead by 34 seconds in a race they would win by 2:18.

Tom Whidden described that victory as their "finest hour." The score was 4-2. Conner would also win the next two races, making the score 4-4, on April 28, in the best-of-thirteen series.

In tennis, the ninth game in a set is critical. The ninth race in the defense trials, with the score tied at four, proved critical, too. Here, the lead changed four times. On the first leg, Conner was leading. Then *America³* passed him and rounded the weather mark 14 seconds ahead. On the run, Conner had a bit more speed and got ahead again to round the leeward mark in front by nine seconds.

On the next weather leg, *America³*, on port, tacked inside and ahead of *Stars & Stripes* very near the mark (see right-hand figure). At this point it seemed as if *Stars & Stripes* had slightly overstood the mark, but exhaust from *America³* was beginning to hurt. Conner's boat began to sag off the layline and slow precipitously. Conner went down to the low-side wheel and watched in frustration and admiration as *America³* began what would prove to be her inevitable march into the America's Cup match.

The wind went left at this point, favoring *America³*. The shift, combined with the bad air from *America³*, caused Conner's sails to luff. *Stars & Stripes* practically stopped. With no speed, Conner tacked away. Melges, however, followed the header down and tacked while maintaining his speed. He tacked back again to round the mark with a 32-second lead. The delta at the finish was 25 seconds for *America³*.

America³ won the next race and, on May 1, with a 5:08 win over *Stars & Stripes*, the right to meet *Il Moro* in the America's Cup match.

Goliath was ready to face the future.

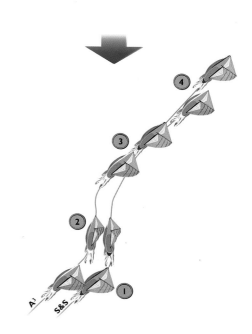

Opposite, America³ *takes her victory lap on May 1. Above, in Position 1,* America³ *starts to pass* Stars & Stripes. *In Position 2,* Stars & Stripes *luffs* America³. America³ *almost stops as a result of the luff.* Stars & Stripes *accelerates for speed in Position 3. With the speed,* Stars & Stripes *moves ahead and to weather in Position 4.*

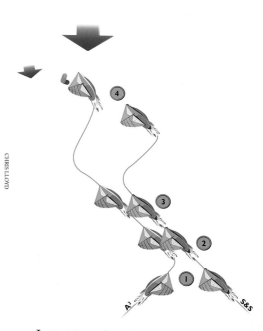

In Position 1, America³ *tacks inside and ahead of* Stars & Stripes, *which seems to have overstood the mark. In Position 2, bad air from* America³ *has begun to hurt* Stars & Stripes. *In Position 3, there is a big windshift to the left, or counter-clockwise, favoring* America³. *Between the shift and* America³*'s bad air,* Stars & Stripes *practically stops and is forced to tack.* America³ *follows the header down and tacks with speed to round the mark ahead — Position 4.*

CHAPTER SIX

THE LOUIS VUITTON CUP

Challenger Races for the America's Cup

New Zealand, pictured opposite, finished second to Il Moro, in the Louis Vuitton Cup. Before the Italians played the "bowsprit card," New Zealand's record was 29–6, the best in competition.

THE LOUIS VUITTON CUP, to choose an America's Cup challenger, began on January 25, 1992, with eight entries: *Spirit of Australia, España, Tre Kronor, Challenge Australia, Nippon, Ville de Paris, New Zealand,* and *Il Moro di Venezia.* Eighty-five races later, the field was reduced by half: the first four boats were gone. This cruel math continued through the semifinals, which began on March 29 and ended April 9. Gone then were *Nippon,* which had started the round in first place, and *Ville de Paris.*

That left the titans: *Il Moro* and *New Zealand,* to wage war. The Italians had built five boats, the Kiwis, four. Wage war, they did, too, on the racecourse, in the protest room, and before the press.

The Kiwis started strongly, going up 4-1. Needing but one more victory, they seemed to have their arms not merely around the Louis Vuitton Cup but the America's Cup. Then the Italians fanned into flames an issue that had been smoldering for 92 days — the bowsprit on *New Zealand*. They forced the Kiwis to examine their downwind sailing and, apparently, themselves.

Then the Kiwis switched helmsmen, from Rod Davis to Russell Coutts. The Italians recognized the change as a sign of weakness — of confusion — and they grew strong exploiting it.

There is something sad when a machine that has been running perfectly suddenly self-destructs. "The wheels fell off," is how one *New Zealand* crewmember described their free-fall from grace. When the smoke finally cleared, *Il Moro di Venezia*, the Moor of Venice, stood at the top of the mountain.

ROUND ONE

On the first day of the Louis Vuitton Cup, hope sprang eternal. Two nations, Spain and Japan, making their debuts, won. The Japanese posted the fastest time around the racecourse in the four races that day. Spain's *España 92*, skippered by Pedro Campos, a small-boat ace, easily beat *Challenge Australia*. The other races were significant, too. *Spirit of Australia*, designed by Iain Murray, who had designed and skippered *Kookaburra III*, the 1987 defender, led *Il Moro* across the starting line by eight seconds. At the first weather mark, the Australian boat led the eventual Louis Vuitton challenger by 1:07. Downwind, however, design flaws in the Australian boat became apparent. So determined was this group of Australians to win back what they had lost in 1987 that they departed this round early, after four races, to subject their boat to chainsaw surgery.

The best race of the day and, as it turned out, the most significant for the outcome of the Louis Vuitton Cup, was the race between *New Zealand* and *Ville de Paris*. Marc Bouet, starting helmsman on the Marc Pajot-skippered French boat, won the start and led the New Zealanders at the first mark by 19 seconds. On the first run, when the Kiwis made use of their bowsprit to jibe, the French raised a protest flag. While no one realized it that innocent January day, the seeds of the Kiwi destruction were sewn at that moment.

Yves Carcelle is president of Louis Vuitton Malletier. Opposite, Il Moro di Venezia, ITA-25, and Spirit of Australia *jockey for position before the start.*

The French would drop their protest, but Paul Cayard, skipper of *Il Moro*, would not be so kind the next day. On January 26, Cayard won the start by pushing *New Zealand* over the line prematurely. A windshift, however, allowed the Kiwis to take the lead on the first weather leg. Then three odd things happened: While leading, the Kiwis badly miscalculated a layline and were forced to tack two extra times to round. The Italians were only 12 seconds behind at the rounding, when they should have trailed by considerably more. Then the Kiwis did a bear-away set at the mark, heading for the right side. The Italians did a jibe set and headed left, where the wind was fresher. The Kiwis set too small a spinnaker for the very light breezes, then failed to cover the Italians.

The Italians won the race easily, by 2:14, then charged the Kiwis with "sandbagging" — that is, slowing down and making mistakes intentionally, to avoid tipping their hand too early. (Sandbagging is a theme of the modern America's Cup. Usually someone is accusing Dennis Conner of sandbagging.)

More significant, when the New Zealanders jibed their gennaker for the first time,

Above, skippers, shown in the front row, determined pairings for the Louis Vuitton Cup. Behind the table, left to right, are Gunnar Krantz (Tre Kronor), Pedro Campos (España 92), Rod Davis (New Zealand), Chris Dickson (Nippon), Paul Cayard (Il Moro di Venezia), Marc Pajot (Ville de Paris), Phil Thompson (Challenge Australia), and Peter Gilmour (Spirit of Australia).

Louis Vuitton banners decorated downtown San Diego. The company was the sponsor of the Challenger Selection Series. On the following spread Ville de Paris, *left, and* Challenge Australia *are seen in a Bob Grieser photograph.*

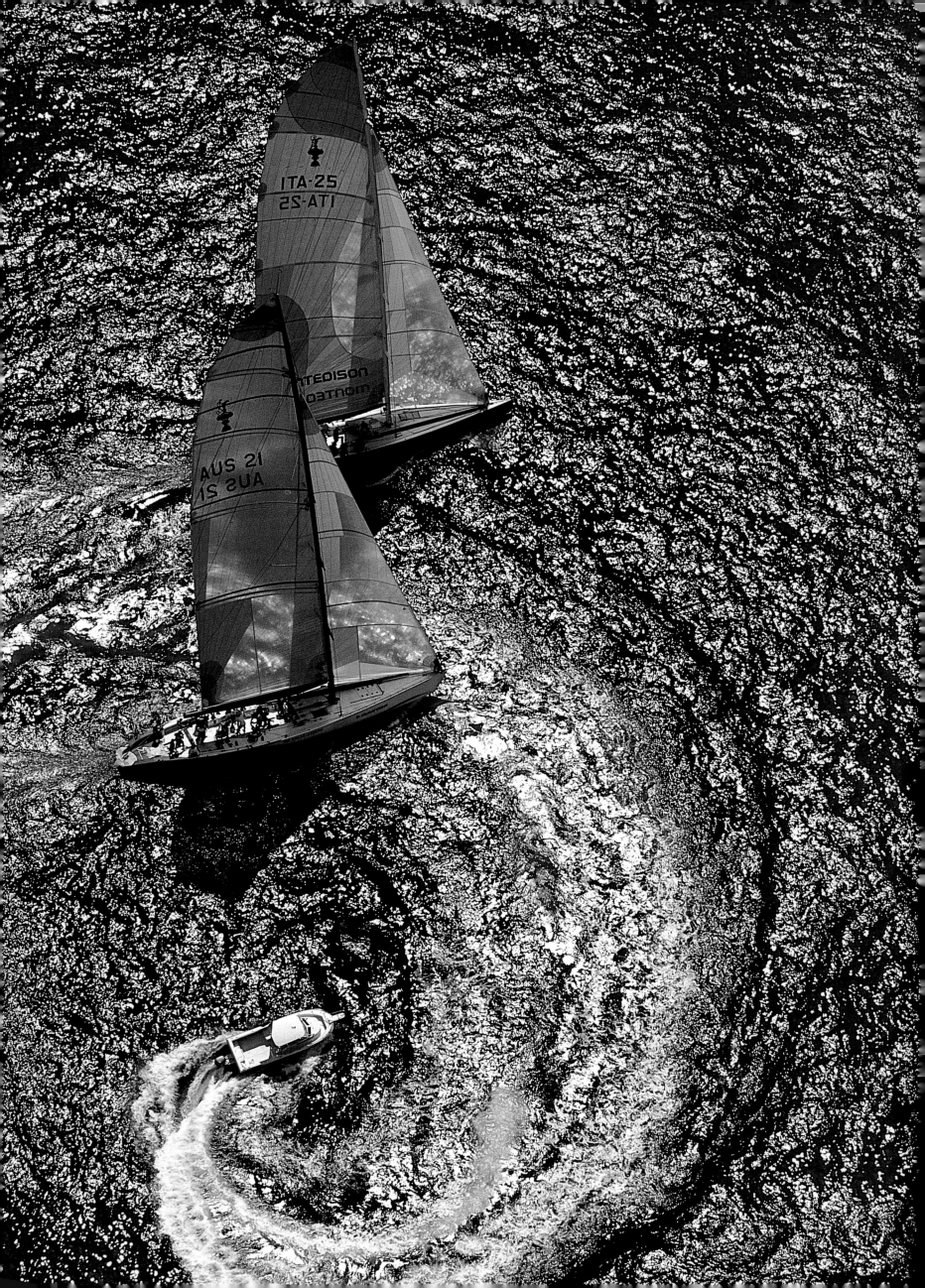

the Italians protested. Said Cayard, "We're not protesting the bowsprit. We're protesting how the Kiwis are using it for an advantage when maneuvering." The Louis Vuitton Cup jury that night dismissed the protest. Still, the time bomb was ticking.

Round one ended with the Kiwis tied for first place; their only loss was to the Italians. The big surprise, however, was that they were tied with the Japanese. In third place was the French *Ville de Paris*, tied with *Il Moro di Venezia*. Then came *Spirit of Australia*, which had won three races before dropping out for modifications, *España*, which had won two, *Tre Kronor*, and *Challenge Australia*.

Tre Kronor *sailed for Sweden. On the opposite page* New Zealand, NZL 20, *and* Ville de Paris *sail overlapped on a reach. On day six of the second round robin,* New Zealand *beat* Ville de Paris *by a scant eight seconds.*

ROUND TWO

The first day of the second round was postponed as a storm lashed San Diego. The next day, February 16, *Spirit of Australia*, vastly modified by the addition of a forked keel and the elimination of her aft rudder, met *New Zealand*. During the pre-start maneuvering there was a minor collision between the boats. The umpires' call went against the Australians, who were cited for tacking too close. The Kiwis went on to win by 12:12 in light and shifty winds.

Jean-Marc Loubier is director of communications for Louis Vuitton Malletier.

In the second day of racing, February 17, the Italians beat the French by a razor-thin 11 seconds. The first time these two boats had met in the first round, the margin of victory had been 25 seconds for the French. In this start Cayard was over the line early by one second. The French led at the first weather mark by 20 seconds and at the leeward mark by 21 seconds — that would be the greatest separation of the day. Through the seventh mark — the last weather mark before the run to the finish — the French held on to a seven-second lead. On the final run they lost a spinnaker guy and were forced to jibe away to gain control of the sail. This gave the lead and the win to the Italians.

On day six, *Tre Kronor* won her first real race against *Challenge Australia* by 6:59; her previous victory had been a formality when this same boat had withdrawn for modifications.

On February 23, the scheduled last day of racing in the second round, *España 92* beat *Spirit of Australia* by 1:25. This left the Spanish in fifth place and the Australians in sixth. The race between *Nippon* and *Il Moro* proved very interesting. The Italian boat won the race by 11 seconds; however, the first leeward mark had drifted out of position, and the Japanese protested. The jury offered to split the points, but neither group favored that. So they sailed the race again, and this time the Italians won by 46 seconds.

New Zealand *starts a race in the Challenger Selection Series. Until the very end, this boat was dominant in the trials.*

By the end of the second round the Kiwis led the series. The Italians displaced the Japanese and took over second place, the Japanese dropped to third, and the French were in fourth.

On March 5, between rounds two and three, the America's Cup International Jury — not to be confused with the Louis Vuitton Cup Jury — had its say on the bowsprit issue. Asked jointly by the Challenger of Record Committee (CORC) and the America's Cup Organizing Committee (ACOC) for an opinion, the America's Cup (AC) jury, headed by Goran Petersson, said that to attach the gennaker sheet to the bowsprit was

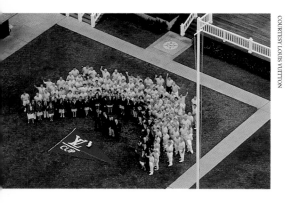

The Louis Vuitton Cup Media
Center staff and the Challenger of
Record Committee (CORC) staff
and volunteers pose at the South-
western Yacht Club. Right, New
Zealand, the red boat, races España
92 under a dramatic sky.

a violation of IYRU Rule 64. While in theory the AC jury had no elevated status at this point, in practice it did, because it would be the jury judging the America's Cup match. Yet the Louis Vuitton Cup jury refused to be bound by the AC jury's decision. Peter Blake, head of the New Zealand syndicate, was incensed. "Here we are contesting the most prestigious sailing regatta in the world, but the referees can't agree on the rules. Where does that leave the competitors?"

ROUND THREE

On day one of the third round, the French dispatched the Kiwis. Both boats were over the starting line early. After restarting, *New Zealand* led at the first mark by eight seconds. On the run, the French came toward the mark on port tack; the Kiwis came on starboard tack, with right-of-way at the crossing. However, *Tre Kronor*, trailing in a race that had started 10 minutes before, got in the way, and the Kiwis couldn't press their starboard-tack advantage. When both boats jibed toward the mark for the rounding, it appeared the New Zealanders had an inside overlap, and thus rights. Nevertheless, *Ville de Paris* broke the overlap and rounded ahead.

On the next weather leg, the Kiwis tacked 35 times; the Citizen Watch "delta," or time difference, at the windward mark was seven seconds. On the three reaching legs the Kiwis, trying to comply with the moving bowsprit rulings, jibed their spinnaker without benefit of the bowsprit, and they had trouble. Finally, *Ville de Paris* won the race by 1:21.

For the Italians, the nadir was probably March 11, when the Kiwis beat them by 5:01. Said Cayard, "We're not exactly where we'd like to be, but nobody goes through life unscathed. Today wasn't a good day, but by no means are we throwing in the towel or quitting."

On the second to last day, March 14, *España* had to beat *Il Moro* to survive the cut. It was not to be: *Il Moro* won the race by 2:14. Said Bruno Troublé, media director for Louis Vuitton, "In my opinion, no group was better at starting-line tactics than Pedro Campos and the crew on *España 92*. A very impressive first effort."

The semifinals were set: *Nippon*, which went unbeaten in this round, finished first; *New Zealand*, which lost to the Japanese and the French in this segment, was second. Then came *Il Moro* and *Ville de Paris*.

SEMIFINALS

Japan was in first place, and the Japanese boat was unique — the only boat in this America's Cup competition to sail with a forward "canard" rudder as well as an aft rudder. On March 29, at the start of the Louis Vuitton semifinal round, Chris Dickson, *Nippon*'s skipper, saw the flipper of a diver on the start of the tow out to the racecourse. The diver was caught and arrested. It proved to be a budget consultant for the French syndicate. His underwater reconnaissance was described as unauthorized and a response to a dare. After being fined $40, he was fired by the French syndicate and unceremoniously sent home to France.

Perhaps because of the distraction, both the French and the Japanese lost on the first day of the races, to the Italians and Kiwis, respectively. The French came roaring back the next day with a 1:46 victory over *New Zealand*. Starting helmsman Marc

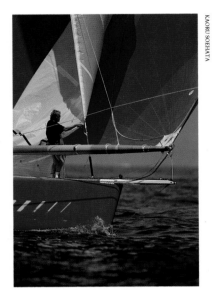

KAORU SOEHATA

The bowsprit on New Zealand *received inordinate attention from the other challengers. It eventually sewed the seeds of the Kiwis' destruction. On the opposite page, crewmembers on* Nippon *work the winches.* Nippon, *while eliminated in the semifinals, had an extraordinary run in her debut in the 1992 Cup.*

BOB GRIESER

Security was a reality — often a grim reality — of the 1992 America's Cup. The Kiwis caught a spy swimming under their boat; so, too, did the Japanese. On the following spread, the titans, Il Moro, *to leeward and ahead, and* New Zealand, *sail upwind in a Carlo Borlenghi photograph.*

Bouet made a port-tack start and crossed the line with speed near the committee-boat end. *New Zealand* was going slower in the middle of the line. The wind went right, favoring the French, who led by 2:30 at the first mark. The Citizen Watch delta would climb as high as 3:42 for the French, who showed dazzling downwind speed. *Nippon*, meanwhile, lost her second race in a row, this one to *Il Moro*, by 2:04. In the third race, on April 1, *Nippon* came unstuck. Her aft carbon-fiber rudderpost crumbled while she was leading the French.

Day four of the semifinals was most dramatic. *Ville de Paris* collided with *Nippon* as the latter was tacking. The result was a huge gash on the bow of the French boat. Had it not been for the crash-box bulkhead, the boat might well have sunk. It seemed a simple "tacking-too-close" call in the French boat's favor; however, the umpires cited the French under Rule 35: "The right-of-way yacht shall not alter course so as to prevent the other yacht from keeping clear." Videotape of the incident supported the umpires' call. After a penalty turn, the French lost to the Japanese by 2:00.

That day, the Italians led the Kiwis by 13 seconds at the third windward mark. It was less of a lead than it seemed, since on the previous run the New Zealanders had made up 23 seconds. Nearing the finish line, the Italians were still ahead. Cayard, skipper of *Il Moro*, jibed onto starboard for the finish line (see figure to right). The Kiwis came at them on port tack, then jibed onto starboard on the Italian boat's weather quarter. Cayard luffed *New Zealand* away from the finish line, but then lost his luffing rights when *New Zealand* achieved mast-abeam. Cayard jibed to port for the finish. The Kiwis immediately jibed, too. As the inside boat has room at a mark, the Kiwis seemed well-positioned to win. Rod Davis "shot the line," turning more directly downwind at the last second to use the boat's momentum to finish more quickly, and *New Zealand* was declared the winner by one second — the second closest race in the history of the Louis Vuitton Cup. However, the umpires said *New Zealand* had touched the mark — a violation of the racing rules. That took the victory away. The contact with the mark was not obvious, and the decision was hugely controversial.

The next two days of racing saw the spiritual if not yet the numerical demise of the Japanese. On day five, April 5, Dickson sailed a brilliant second weather leg and had to duck the Kiwis when crossing on port tack. When a port-tacker ducks a starboard-tacker, there is always the possibility of a slam-dunk maneuver (see figure to right), and when Dickson ducked, the Kiwis tacked onto *Nippon*'s weather bow. Dickson thought there was room to tack back to starboard. There wasn't, and the umpires cited Dickson for an illegal luff. The result was a 270-degree penalty turn and a loss.

The next day, the Japanese broke their boom while maneuvering before the start and sailed the race against the Italians without one. Even then, they only lost by 1:53.

On day seven the French raced the Italians. The Italians were 30 seconds early for the start, and Code flag "X," signaling an individual recall, went up immediately, along with the yellow flag denoting *Il Moro*. However, the French, too, had been over early — by one second — but their blue recall flag wasn't raised until about 25 seconds later. By then, the French were long gone. Disputing an advisory over the radio that they had started improperly, the French flew a protest flag of their own. An hour into this confused affair, the race committee, realizing its mistake, called the race off. The

Opposite, Nippon, *in the fore-ground, leads* Il Moro. *Above, on day four of the semifinals*, Ville de Paris *collided with* Nippon. *On the following spread is a Franco Pace photograph of* Nippon.

In *Position 1,* New Zealand *jibed to weather of* Il Moro. *In Position 2,* Il Moro *luffed the Kiwi boat. In Position 3, the boats have jibed for the finish. In Position 4, the Kiwis "shot the line," but the umpires ruled they had touched the mark.*

In *Position 1,* Nippon *(JPN 26) on port tack, ducked* New Zealand. New Zealand *then tacked onto port to execute the "slam-dunk" maneuver. Chris Dickson, skipper of* Nippon, *however, tried to escape it by luffing and then tacking (Position 2). He was cited for an illegal luff.*

restart was at three in the afternoon, and *Il Moro* led at every mark, securing herself a place in the finals.

On April 8, 1992, the Kiwis beat the French by a huge 3:30. The Louis Vuitton finals would be between *Il Moro* and *New Zealand*.

The French deserved a better exit than this. *Ville de Paris*, designed by Philippe Briand, was an extraordinary boat. Had Briand been given the opportunity to refine his work again with a fourth boat, the results might have been very different.

At the end, *Ville de Paris* skipper Marc Pajot said, "I have offered assistance to the remaining syndicates if they need it." The Italians would take the French up on that offer. The assistance would come in the form of advice on gennaker design. The luffs, or leading edges, of the gennakers on the Italian boat were positive — or curved outward. The luffs of the gennakers on the French boats were negative. In copying the French designs, the Italians changed from being 20 seconds slower than the Kiwis downwind to 20 seconds faster. This 40-second improvement was enough to turn an uneven boat into a super boat.

LOUIS VUITTON FINALS

The Kiwis won the first race of the Louis Vuitton finals on April 19, 1992, by 1:32. Cayard and company made a series of errors, from being late at the start by a whopping 18 seconds to not having the correct gennaker aboard.

The second race was the closest in Louis Vuitton history, since the delta between the boats never exceeded 19 seconds. The Italians took the start by one second and were two boatlengths ahead at the first crossing. Cayard worked the right side but Rod Davis, skipper of *New Zealand*, sailed on the left and crossed ahead. At the first mark, the Kiwis led by 13 seconds. At the second mark, they led by five seconds — the Italians showed that they were now faster than the Kiwis downwind. At the end of the second weather leg, *New Zealand* led by eight seconds. At this rounding *New Zealand*, on starboard tack, was slow. *Il Moro*, on port, had to slow to keep from fouling *New Zealand*. The two red boats sailed the reach marks as if they were joined bow to stern. The delta at the fourth and fifth marks was nine seconds; at the sixth it was 12 seconds.

On the final weather leg, the boats split tacks. *New Zealand* went right on port tack, and *Il Moro* went left on starboard. When the two boats came together again, the Italian boat had to duck *New Zealand*. Davis tacked into the slam-dunk position, but Cayard dropped down for an instant and had sufficient room to tack away. Again Cayard went left on starboard tack as *New Zealand* continued right on port. When the boats tacked and came together again, Davis again tried for a slam dunk, but Italy again successfully avoided it. A third time they came together, and the Kiwis executed what appeared to be a perfect slam dunk (see figure to left). Davis pointed at Cayard's mast, signaling mast-abeam. This would prevent the Italians, to leeward, from luffing. *Il Moro* immediately raised a protest flag, claiming the Kiwis' mast-abeam call was premature. The incident was green-flagged by the umpires, indicating no foul. Nevertheless, Cayard just managed to get his boat into what is called the lee-bow position. This meant the Italians were now giving the Kiwis bad air, and the Kiwis were forced to tack away. They were now behind.

It wasn't over, however. When the boats came together again, *New Zealand*, on

*C*hris Dickson, *left, skipper of* Nippon*; Marc Pajot, skipper of* Ville de Paris, *and their crews receive trophies and Citizen watches before exiting the Louis Vuitton Cup after the semifinal round. This left the playing field to* Il Moro *and* New Zealand. *Opposite is Pajot's* Ville de Paris. *On the following spread is a Carlo Borlenghi photograph of* Il Moro.

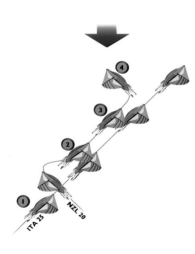

*A*s Il Moro *(ITA 25) ducked* New Zealand. *(Position 1), the Kiwi boat seemed to execute a perfect slam dunk (Position 2). If the Kiwis could have kept their bow in front of* Il Moro, *they would have been ahead and in control. However, in Position 3,* Il Moro *was able to get her nose in front of* New Zealand. *Now in the "lee-bow" position,* Il Moro *was hurting* New Zealand *with her bad air.* New Zealand *was forced to tack away (Position 4).*

BOB GREISER

On Sunday, April 26, Paul Cayard, in the Il Moro vest, told a press conference he wasn't satisfied with how New Zealand used its bowsprit, or with the rulings about its legality by the Louis Vuitton Cup jury. Others on the stage include, left to right, Bruce Farr, New Zealand's designer; Sir Michael Fay, the syndicate head; Bruno Troublé, moderator; Raul Gardini, head of the Il Moro syndicate; and Gabriele Rafenelli, the administrative director.

CARLO BORLENGHI

Bruce Farr, designer of New Zealand, attempts to answer the question whether the bowsprit exerted outward pressure — a violation of Rule 64.4 — or downward pressure, which, in his opinion, wasn't a violation. "The test of whether there is a downward pressure exerted on the spinnaker pole by the foreguy is that if you ease the foreguy, the pole will lift, and that is precisely what happens," he said.

tack of the gennaker was being controlled by a line from the tack of the gennaker through a block near the end of a bowsprit." This, it said, was a violation of CORC Rule 8.9. However, instead of disqualifying the Kiwis and awarding the race to *Il Moro*, the jury annulled the race. The score returned to 3-1 for *New Zealand*.

Cayard was not mollified; at the very least he wanted the victory, not a resail, and he wanted the jury to address Rule 64, too. On Sunday, April 26, at a packed 8:00 a.m. press conference, he said, "First, this jury, in my thinking, is consistently in New Zealand's camp on this issue."

Cayard disclosed that the Kiwis had made a video of how they were using the bowsprit and presented it privately to the CORC jury, who approved its use. This was highly irregular. He also pointed out that a member of the jury, which made the decision, was the father of a crewmember on *New Zealand*. Moreover, he said, the Louis Vuitton Cup was being raced under different rules (CORC Rule 8.9) than would be used for the America's Cup match. This called into question the credibility of the entire challenger-selection series. Indeed, under America's Cup rules, all CORC rules, such as 8.9, must be submitted for approval to the San Diego Yacht Club. In the case of amended CORC Rule 8.9, this was never done.

Paul Cayard continued: "The point of this whole thing is that the gennaker on *New Zealand* is being flown by a rope that goes directly from the bowsprit to the tack of the sail. The rope which controls the tack of the sail is not led through the spinnaker pole."

At this same press conference, Raul Gardini, head of the Il Moro di Venezia syndicate, told the assembled crowd that "*New Zealand* has been racing in the Louis Vuitton Cup regatta with an unsportsmanlike manner and with the same unsportsmanlike attitude using this bowsprit in this way."

It had been a rough night for Paul Cayard in the protest room, and a rough press conference. Nevertheless, the Italians won race six later that day by 43 seconds. Cayard protested this race, too. The protest was based on how *New Zealand* was carrying its spinnaker when "straight-line sailing." That night, with both skippers again in attendance, the Louis Vuitton Cup jury dismissed the protest.

This was a pivotal moment in the history of the 1992 America's Cup. The San Diego Yacht Club, in truth, could have fanned the flames themselves. They might have waited until *New Zealand* was named challenger — which looked likely at this point — and then asked the match jury to decide if this was a proper challenger or not, since *New Zealand*, in effect, had qualified under different rules. Due to extraordinary behind-the-scenes maneuvering by ACOC's Tom Ehman and CORC's Dr. Stan Reid, calm heads prevailed. The next day, the jury and Dr. Reid faced the press in a conference orchestrated by Bruno Troublé of Louis Vuitton.

Yacht-racing juries are like Supreme Court justices — their decisions are rarely subjected to direct questions. "I received a lot of pressure from many people not to hold this press conference or the previous one," said Troublé. Nevertheless he went ahead with it for what he believed to be for the good of the event.

Dr. Reid spoke candidly and with dignity: "The Challenger of Record Committee

COURTESY LOUIS VUITTON

Ernie Taylor was executive director of CORC. Opposite, the finalists spar before the start of the fourth race.

Opposite is the finish of the second race in the finals, in which Il Moro, *with the white spinnaker, beat* New Zealand *by one second. This was the closest race in the history of the Louis Vuitton Cup, because the delta never exceeded 19 seconds. Above are the three winners of the Louis Vuitton Cup, right to left: Paul Cayard in 1992, Dennis Conner in 1987, and John Bertrand in 1983.*

has to date issued five amendments to the conditions (CORC rules). None of these has been formally presented to the San Diego Yacht Club, although they have been in public demand ever since they were written. The fact that they have not been presented to the San Diego Yacht Club is an error of mine..."

He also said that over the previous night, CORC rule 8.9 had been amended again. It now followed the exact words from the March 5 interpretation by the America's Cup jury. "*New Zealand* has told me that they will be complying with this amendment in today's race."

All was going well until Graeme Owens, chairman of the Louis Vuitton Cup jury, said, "We do not believe there is a change in the meaning. There has been a change in wording to keep a number of people happy." At which point Barbara Lloyd, of the New York *Times*, asked, "I am confused. If the change in the wording does not change the meaning, then why are the New Zealanders changing the way that they are sailing today?" What followed was a strange colloquy.

Bruno Troublé was director of the Louis Vuitton Cup Media Organization.

"Who said they are changing today?" Owens asked. "Stan Reid," said Lloyd. "Well," replied Owens, "obviously Stan knows something that we don't."

The New Zealanders did change the way they flew their gennaker that day, April 29. The issue was apparently becoming a huge distraction.

The Kiwis also changed skippers later that day, from Rod Davis to Russell Coutts. Davis responded to his demotion with extraordinary dignity. "This is not the Rod Davis show or anyone else's show. It is the Kiwi team's..."

It might have made sense for Coutts to start the boat and for Davis to steer it after that, as Marc Bouet did for Mark Pajot on *Ville de Paris* or David Dellenbaugh did for Buddy Melges on *America³* — but that didn't happen.

Steering *New Zealand*, with its two trim tabs and no rudder, was about as intuitive as steering a helicopter. Coutts, while a talented and aggressive match racer, had only steered *New Zealand* three times in actual races. It was no surprise that he had some difficulties when called upon in the final races. Coutts and *New Zealand* lost the next two races and on April 30, the Louis Vuitton Cup.

Hindsight, of course, is always clear. Had the Kiwis changed their bowsprit technique between rounds two and three, when it became obvious that they wouldn't be allowed to use it that way in the America's Cup match, they might well have won the Louis Vuitton Cup *and* the America's Cup.

In the dénouement, the Kiwis protested the Italians under Rule 75, the Fair Sailing rule. The flash point was, apparently, Raul Gardini's implication that the Kiwis had been cheating. On the way in after winning the final race, Gardini went aboard the Kiwi tender and offered his apologies to Sir Michael Fay. Sir Michael accepted it, but wanted it done publicly. He told Bruno Troublé that he was willing to go back to *New Zealand* as a "loser," but not as a "cheat." At the press conference that evening, Gardini offered a formal apology. Sir Michael nodded to Stan Reid, signaling that he was dropping the protest. After four months and 119 races, Reid presented the Louis Vuitton Cup to *Il Moro di Venezia*.

Sir Michael Fay, right, offers his congratulations to Paul Cayard and Raul Gardini for winning the Louis Vuitton Cup match. On the opposite page, Il Moro heads home after winning the right to meet the American defender.

Paul Cayard, Il Moro's skipper, lets loose a Moët champagne shower, celebrating the Italian victory.

Cayard would thrust, and Dellenbaugh would parry, using his adversary's strength and aggressiveness to *America³*'s advantage.

It wasn't just yacht design, however, that accounted for the more reserved prestart maneuvering of *America³*. Dellenbaugh is, by nature, unflappable; Cayard — a disciple of Tom Blackaller — is fiery. Further, an angry Paul Cayard, the *America³* team realized, is a dangerous Paul Cayard. This was a lesson gleaned from Cayard's epic battles with the New Zealanders and the Louis Vuitton Cup jury.

So scrupulously did *America³* follow their plan of peaceful accommodation that America's Cup 1992 almost proved to be the "friendly competition between foreign nations" naively described in the Deed of Gift.

With one minute, 20 seconds before the starting gun of the first race, both boats were on port tack, two boatlengths over the starting line. *Il Moro* tacked first and fell off onto a broad reach to get back to the proper side of the line. *America³*, going two knots slower, made a lumbering turn for the line from behind. Once across the line, *America³* jibed and headed up on port tack for the committee-boat end.

At 30 seconds to the gun, Cayard headed back on starboard tack for the pin end. Cayard, who appeared to be well-stoked with adrenaline at this point, had a head of steam and should have had a great start. If he was going to be early, he had at least a couple of boatlengths before the starting mark to kill time. At the gun, however, he was 16 feet over the starting line — a major misstep — and had to recross. By the time he extricated himself, *Il Moro* was 30 seconds behind at the start. That was the time difference, or delta, at the finish.

At the press conference that evening, Cayard said that they had totally misjudged the current. They had thought it was only half a knot, he said, when it was actually closer to a knot.

RACE TWO

For the second race, on May 10, the wind was light at 8 to 10 knots. *America³*, at the pin end, was across the line first by one second, while *Il Moro*, starting at the committee-boat end, seemed to have the better start on the favored right-hand side of the course. At the first crossing, however, *America³*, using what was beginning to look like better boatspeed, was almost able to cross ahead of the Italian challenger. Had Buddy Melges, the helmsman on *America³* after the start, been bolder, the defender probably could have crossed ahead. Rather than risking a foul, however, Melges tacked into the safe-leeward position. Cayard hung in this untenable position for a minute before tacking away. With the tack, *America³* was ahead, but not in control.

On the second meeting, *America³*, on port tack, tried to get to the favored right-hand side. This time, rather than crossing or tacking into the safe-leeward position, the American defender ducked. With the duck, *Il Moro* was able to execute a perfect slam-dunk maneuver on *America³*. On a long port tack, *Il Moro* controlled the defender to the layline, rounding the first mark with a 33-second advantage. This was the exact move *Il Moro* had used against *New Zealand* in the second race of the Louis Vuitton Finals; *Il Moro* had won that race by one second.

The American boat, with a bigger spinnaker, gained on the downwind leg by sailing a lower and faster course. Lower *and* faster, as sailors know, is a devastating

Opposite, after the slam dunk on the first leg of race two, Il Moro *controlled the defender to the layline. The challenger led at the first mark by 32 seconds and at the finish by 3 seconds — the closest race in the history of the America's Cup. Above is a spinnaker drop on* Il Moro.

Above, America³ *hoists a "Cuben-fiber" headsail — the material was proprietary to this syndicate and was reportedly lighter and lower stretch than Kevlar — a sailmaking standard. On the following spread is a Franco Pace photo showing* America³ *biding her time to weather of* Il Moro *before a start.*

was obvious that Cayard and *Il Moro* could win in the clinches. Could they win when contact wasn't possible?

It was a painful loss for *America³* but a gain in terms of information. First, the defender had been told to avoid downspeed tacking duels, but they had engaged in one on the final weather leg and gained considerably until falling into a hole. Also, while their jibes were undistinguished, to put it kindly, their spinnaker was much bigger and, as such, less stable and much harder to manage in the light wind. "We gained on them in the jibing duel," said David Dellenbaugh, although he admitted that the last jibe had probably cost them the race. Most important, the crew of *America³* now realized that they enjoyed a comfortable speed advantage downwind. "Despite the loss, we had a strong sense that we could beat those guys," said Dellenbaugh.

RACE THREE

For the third race, on May 12, the sun made its first appearance in the America's Cup match. Nevertheless, by day's end, the sun was beginning to set on the Moor of Venice. This day, the wind was blowing 10 knots from 275 degrees, and the seas were smooth. Smooth seas should have favored *Il Moro*, as they had favored *Stars & Stripes* in the defender trials.

With 2:20 to go before the start, *Il Moro* led *America³* to the line on starboard tack. By leading back, Cayard had the option to go to either end. It appeared that there was more wind on the left side of the course; however, Cayard let *America³* sail to leeward of him, conceding the left. With 50 seconds before the gun, both boats were over the line at about the middle of it. Cayard tacked to port, and *America³* bore away on starboard to return.

America³ started at the favored left-hand end on starboard tack with speed, *Il Moro* started at the committee-boat end, with a two-second lead, on port tack.

Then the wind shifted left, or counterclockwise, by 10 degrees, favoring *America³*. There was also more velocity on the left-hand side, and *America³* took the lead, rounding the first mark 47 seconds ahead of the challenger. By the finish she had increased that lead to 1:58. The score was now 2-1 for *America³*.

The race had its dramatic moments, a number of which were provided by ESPN's "Scuba-Cam." The television network had equipped a diver with a camera and tethered him to an ESPN boat near the first reaching mark. The low angle was interesting, but the cameraman was bobbing unsteadily and sickeningly in the waves. There was considerable current this day, and the cameraman had drifted onto the race-course. Dellenbaugh, tactician on *America³*, noticed the diver first in the midst of the mark-rounding. "I told Bill, 'You're not rounding the mark, you're rounding that yellow head.'"

As *Il Moro* rounded a minute and four seconds later, her bow wave tossed the cameraman aside and rolled him over and over like a body-surfer in the trough of a breaker. There was a brief flash of *Il Moro*'s red hull streaking past at 12 knots. It was much too close for comfort. At the post-race press conference, Cayard compared the problems of Scuba-Cam to his premature start in the first race. "He's kind of like me. He doesn't know about current."

At the press conference, Cayard was also asked about Peter Gilmour's prediction

Opposite is the classic America's Cup crossing photograph. Above, on land, at the tip of Point Loma, there was a sizable audience for America's Cup viewing.

Interest was intense at sea, too. Here America³ heads past the lighthouse at the tip of Point Loma after a victory over Il Moro. On the following spread is a Bob Grieser photograph of America³ leading Il Moro in the third race.

crew came aboard and concluded that the only possible solution was to lash the mast to keep it from moving. Leaving that prescription, they got off the boat before the 10-minute gun sounded, as required, and two regular crewmembers went belowdecks to wrestle with the problem.

Then, with eight minutes to go before the start, the mainsail on *America³* ripped at the luff. While this is a low-load area, in the disturbed airflow behind the mast, bowman Jerry Kirby was nevertheless sent aloft to repair the sail with tape. Now three of the racing crew of 16 were otherwise engaged. It was a windy 12 knots, and David Dellenbaugh remembers wondering, "Where is everybody?"

Cayard, seeing a wounded opponent and hoping to issue a *coup de grace*, engaged *America³*. At 3:59 before the start, Cayard, who had been to windward and behind *America³*, swerved behind her transom to get to leeward and, apparently, to jibe. With this precipitous maneuver, however, the top two carbon-fiber battens in *Il Moro*'s mainsail broke. The Italians, the only challengers with a carbon fiber mainsail, had had this problem at least two other times. Broken battens are a much more serious problem than a mere tear in the luff: Along with a loss of proper sailshape in the unsupported area comes the potential for the shattered pieces to rip the sail. Sailing with broken carbon-fiber battens is like trying to contain broken glass in a flexing envelope.

Dellenbaugh was close enough to *Il Moro* to hear the battens shatter. He looked up at the Italian's mainsail and then saw that Cayard had followed his eyes aloft. Dellenbaugh looked up again at the mainsail, to be sure he had made his point. They were posturing like gunslingers. All the moment lacked was the eerie music from a Clint Eastwood western. Said Dellenbaugh, "It was a mind-game."

Again Dellenbaugh wanted the left side of the course and again he got it. On the first crossing, *America³*, on port tack, probably could have crossed *Il Moro*, but opted to tack into the lee-bow position. On the second meeting, the American defender easily crossed and tacked on top to cover. The boats were even in speed on the first windward leg. Perhaps these conditions were to *Il Moro*'s liking, or perhaps, since the wind built on the first leg, *America³* wasn't able to shape her mainsail to the changing conditions due to the broken mast ram.

At the top mark, with *America³* on starboard tack and *Il Moro* on port, less than 10 feet separated the two boats. *America³* crossed ahead of *Il Moro* and then tacked just to windward of her. *Il Moro* flew a protest flag, claiming the American boat had tacked too close. The judges green-flagged the protest. The Citizen Watch delta at the first mark was 18 seconds in favor of *America³*.

After the three reaching legs, which Bill Koch steered, the defender was ahead by 39 seconds. On the last weather leg, Cayard whittled the lead back 15 seconds, to a 24-second delta. On the final leg, Buddy Melges steered *America³* downwind to the finish. Seconds before crossing the line, in answer to all who had criticized his steering since the first races in January, Koch staged a mock-fight with Melges for the helm.

At 2:52 on Saturday afternoon, May 16, 1992, a gun sounded for *America³*. *Il Moro* crossed the line 44 seconds later. The XXVIII Defense of the America's Cup was history.

Over the five-race series, the average time difference between the two boats had been 47 seconds — the closest America's Cup ever.

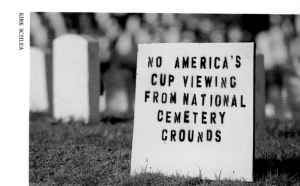

Above, spectators were finally required to abandon the view from the National Cemetery on Point Loma overlooking the racecourse. Opposite, America³ was simply faster than the challenger. Koch's 4–1 victory in the America's Cup match is all the more amazing when you consider his two boats, Jayhawk and USA 2, finished sixth and tied for seventh, respectively in the 1991 International America's Cup Class (IACC) World Champion-ship. Il Moro finished first at that competition.

Buddy Melges, a helmsman on America³, meets the press with his granddaughter after winning an America's Cup race. Melges, age 62, is the first man to win an Olympic gold medal and the America's Cup.

America's Cup — indeed the New World of sailing. Eight years after Koch took up sailing he won its most coveted prize and

T H E R E   I S   N O   S E C O N D

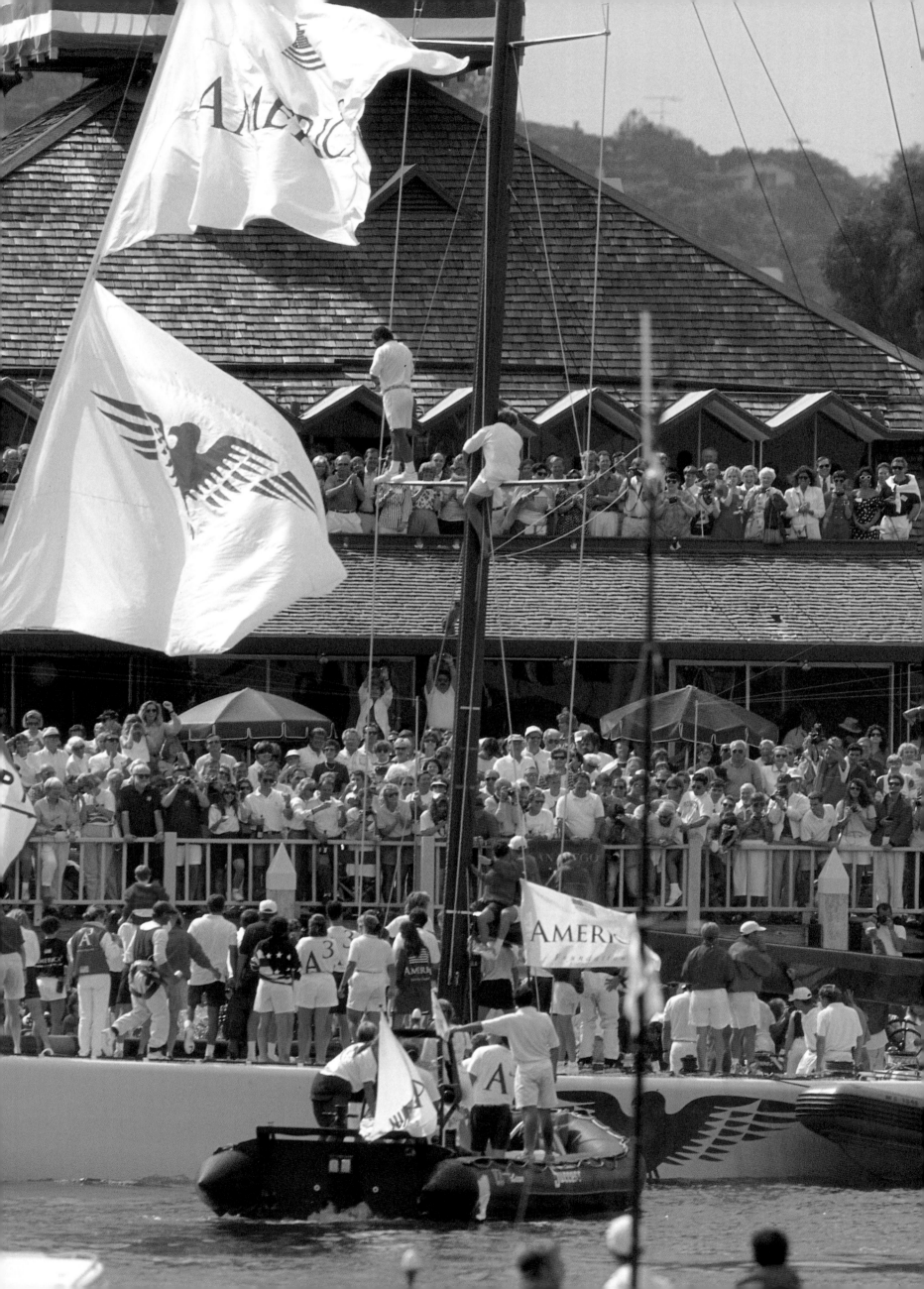

argue with him. "Besides," he added, "if I'm arranging the bulk of the financing, I'll do as I damn well please."

Bill Koch knew he wasn't good enough to win the America's Cup with a slow boat or even a merely competitive boat, so he set out to design and build the fastest boat in San Diego. In the America's Cup, the distance between saying you're out to build the fastest boat and actually doing it is interplanetary. It took Alan Bond four campaigns to win the America's Cup. Koch was successful in his first.

Koch described 1992 as "a tremendous growth period for me." He was awkward at times, sometimes more cerebral than physically agile, sometimes too talkative, sometimes too remote. But he was a fighter of world-class proportions. As those who know him well will attest, the quickest way to be proven wrong is to tell Bill Koch what he can't do.

If Koch had by his own admission a loveless childhood, he is now a man determined not to make the same mistakes. At the press conference following his victory, Koch was asked if he would return in 1995. "Ask my son whether he'll let me do it," he said. Six-year-old Wyatt, sitting comfortably in the embrace of his father, said, "No!" When asked why not, Wyatt said, without any of the introspection of his father, "It's too long!"

Of course, there is a "second" in the America's Cup. At that Sunday-morning ceremony in cheerless May weather — what the locals describe as the "June-gloom" — appeared Raul Gardini and Paul Cayard, syndicate head and skipper, respectively, of the Italian challenger, *Il Moro di Venezia*, which lost to *America³* in five races. Cayard, who is an American, had been called a "mercenary" and a "soldier of fortune." Nevertheless, Cayard and Gardini had had a sailing relationship and then a friendship long before Gardini set his sights on the America's Cup.

The America's Cup was established to be a "friendly competition between foreign countries." However, in a world where boundaries are being redrawn almost daily and economic, political, and cultural borders are blurring, the soldier-of-fortune charge sounded hollow. The current rule about nationality is that competitors need either a passport of the country they are representing or a principal residence there beginning at least two years before the event. Cayard conformed easily to the second rule.

Even Cayard's critics could not fail to be moved as he translated Raul Gardini's Italian into English: "We've lived this challenge as a culture. We've spoken for many, many hours how it came for me, an Italian, and he, an American, to be together. We found out how important it was that there were no barriers, and what we were doing for ourselves and our team..." At this point, a tear filled Cayard's eye, and he had to stop before plowing ahead. By any measure, Paul Pierre Cayard was no mercenary. He finished second in the 1992 America's Cup and did it with extraordinary dignity.

THE FUTURE: AMERICA'S CUP XXIX AND BEYOND

Despite his son's protestations, will Bill Koch return in 1995? Will Raul Gardini or Sir Michael Fay, head of the New Zealand Challenge, be back? Watch the boats. If Koch sells *America³* or Gardini or Sir Michael sell their last boats, they'll likely be absent when the America's Cup world reconvenes in 1995. Or watch the leases on the compounds in San Diego.

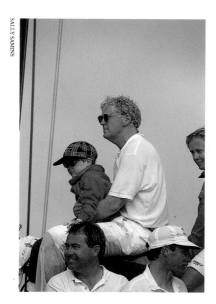

Bill Koch and his son, Wyatt, share a moment together following Koch's win in the America's Cup. Opposite, if the San Diego Yacht Club was ambivalent about Koch in the beginning — as Koch maintained — they were enthusiastic about him at the end.

Paul Cayard, the American skipper of Il Moro, *translates Raul Gardini's Italian into English at the prize-giving ceremony at the San Diego Yacht Club. Cayard's fluency in Italian helped quiet those who had called him a mercenary. On pages 194–195, crew, friends, family, and support staff overload the triumphant* America³ *in this Sally Samins photograph. On pages 196–197, the* America³ *crew celebrates its win with a swim in this photograph by Kirk Schlea.*

KIRK SCHLEA

After the victory, Bill Koch talks to Australian John Bertrand, who won the America's Cup in 1983 as skipper of Australia II. *It was Bertrand who ended the longest winning streak in sports. Opposite, Bill Koch and helmsman Buddy Melges hoist the America's Cup, surrounded by their crew.*

At the very moment *America³* crossed the finish line for the final time, the San Diego Yacht Club was handed two challenges, from the Yacht Club de France in Sète, which sponsored *Ville de Paris* in 1992, and from the Monte Real Club de Yates de Bayona, which sponsored *España 92*. Yacht clubs had 180 days, or until November 19, 1992, to challenge for America's Cup XXIX. According to the America's Cup XXIX protocol, signed by the San Diego Yacht Club, the Royal Perth Yacht Club, and the New York Yacht Club, the present and former trustees of the Cup, the match itself is scheduled to begin "approximately May 1, 1995." It will "be held in the waters of the Pacific Ocean off San Diego…"

What will the America's Cup world look like in 1995? The boats will be the same, according to the protocol. Despite the costs and although the most vocal critic of the class was the winner, Bill Koch, the IACC yacht proved extremely popular. One race in the Cup match was decided by a record three seconds. If you count the race in which *New Zealand* was said not to have finished because she hit the finish-line mark, two races in the Louis Vuitton Cup (LVC) were decided by one second. Four other races in the LVC were decided by less than 18 seconds, after 20 miles of racing. Said Dr. Stan Reid, chairman of the Challenger of Record Committee (CORC), "I think the yacht was superb. The rule was almost perfect. For a first-up effort, the designers ought to be congratulated."

An effort will be made to contain costs. Paragraph 11 of the protocol reads, "… The SDYC will appoint an international committee to recommend ways to reduce costs of future America's Cup campaigns and operations, including the costs of design and construction of the International America's Cup Class." Some cost-saving ideas being considered, said SDYC Commodore Fred Delaney, are "…limiting the number of boats you can build, limiting the number of sails you can build, putting a limit on materials, budgets, [and] the length of the campaigns."

One way to limit the cost is to change the course. The three reaching legs — four, five, and six — require a significant investment in asymmetrical spinnakers. Eliminating one or more of the reaching legs would reduce the costs of a campaign. Costs aren't the only thing, however, when focusing on the course. There were no passing lanes on the reaching legs. *America³*, for example, only passed *Stars & Stripes* once on the reaching Z-legs in four months of racing, spanning 54 races. Passing is what makes the America's Cup interesting to participants and spectators alike.

Under consideration is a six-legged windward-leeward course with the legs about three miles in length. As there are passing lanes upwind and down, this would be compelling. Also, spectator boats could line both sides of the course and get fairly close without interfering much with the wind and the racing. Further, spectators could get even closer if there was a gate in the middle of the leg through which the yachts were required to pass. A more radical idea has also been proposed that each day's racing be the best of three short races, like a three-set tennis match. That would double or triple the most exciting parts of the racing: the start and finish.

The costs of future campaigns will also go down automatically since there are presently 28 IACC boats in existence. Syndicates were starting from scratch for 1992, and the first cycle is always the most costly. Now, used IACC boats can be purchased as trial horses, or, if purchased by a syndicate within the same country that the boat was

designed and built, the boats can be used in actual competition. It is possible, many people think, to run a two- or three-boat syndicate for $20 million and still be competitive.

Other housekeeping matters for 1995 will likely include a single international jury to oversee the defense trials, challenger trials, and the America's Cup match, so that a repeat of "bowsprit-gate" doesn't occur.

On-the-water umpiring proved extremely popular with most syndicates. In almost all cases, there was a winner and a loser when the boats crossed the finish line — not hours later, after protest hearings. Doubtless, there will be pressure to allow umpires to make or change calls after viewing videotaped evidence. Despite such pressure, this seems unlikely, as it hasn't proved successful in other sports.

It also might prove helpful to the umpires if vertical stripes indicating the positions of both mast and helmsman were painted boldly on the hulls of the boats. This would make it easier for the umpires to make "mast-abeam" calls, which are used to curtail luffing. Many protests in 1992 stemmed from premature mast-abeam calls.

Finally, the nationality rules will be addressed, not for the XXIX Defense in 1995, but for the XXX Defense, likely in 1998. Said Commodore Delaney, "I think what we would like to see is a tightening of [the nationality rules] so that you don't have a situation where a hired gun wins it for the United States, and then he goes on to the next match and wins it for Thailand... Then it becomes a helmsman's or skipper's trophy rather than a yacht-club country-challenging trophy."

Whatever refinements are added to the America's Cup competition now, the boats themselves and the personalities that survive the grueling test will remain the cornerstones of the event. These new IACC boats and those who sail them have attracted a new wave of interest in the Cup, while restoking the interest of many who have followed the racing since the days of Vanderbilt and *Ranger*.

The Cup appears to have a gleaming future.

CARLO BORLENGHI

Above, crewmembers change gennakers in the midst of a reaching leg. One way to cut costs in future Cup competitions would be to eliminate one or all three of the reaching legs (four, five, and six), which require a large inventory of expensive and specialized asymmetrical sails. Opposite, with Koch's win, the America's Cup world will return to San Diego and the San Diego Yacht Club in 1995.

CHAPTER NINE

THE OFFICIAL RECORD

Syndicate & Race Results

AMERICA'S CUP XXVIII FINAL
May 9 - May 16, 1992
Best of 7 races

Day 1	Race 1	*America³* def *Il Moro Di Venezia* by	00:30
Day 2	Race 2	*Il Moro Di Venezia* def *America³* by	00:03
Day 3	Race 3	*America³* def *Il Moro Di Venezia* by	01:58
Day 4	Race 4	*America³* def *Il Moro Di Venezia* by	01:04
Day 5	Race 5	*America³* def *Il Moro Di Venezia* by	00:44

THE LOUIS VUITTON CUP
Challenger Races for the 1992 America's Cup

CHALLENGER ROUND ROBIN 1

January 25 - February 3, 1992
Total number of races: 28   Points per win: 1

Day 1	Race 1	*Il Moro* def *Spirit* by 02:23
	Race 2	*New Zealand* def *Ville de Paris* by 00:56
	Race 3	*España 92* def *Challenge* by 02:15
	Race 4	*Nippon* def *Tre Kronor* by 03:30
Day 2	Race 1	*España 92* def *Tre Kronor* by 04:22
	Race 2	*Nippon* def *Challenge* by 08:52
	Race 3	*Il Moro* def *New Zealand* by 02:14
	Race 4	*Ville de Paris* def *Spirit* by 11:00
Day 3	Race 1	*Ville de Paris* def *España 92* by 06:24
	Race 2	*Spirit* def *Tre Kronor* by 13:13
	Race 3	*Nippon* def *Il Moro* by 03:55
	Race 4	*New Zealand* def *Challenge* by 05:03
Day 4	Race 1	*New Zealand* def *Tre Kronor* by 09:38
	Race 2	*Nippon* def *Ville de Paris* by 00:29
	Race 3	*Spirit* def *Challenge* by 02:18
	Race 4	*Il Moro* def *España 92* by 09:46
Day 5	Race 1	*New Zealand* def *Nippon* (DNF)
	Race 2	*Spirit* def *España 92* by 01:50
	Race 3	*Ville de Paris* def *Tre Kronor* by 05:18
	Race 4	*Il Moro* def *Challenge* (DNS)
Day 6	Race 1	*Nippon* def *Spirit* (DNS)
	Race 2	*New Zealand* def *España 92* by 04:16
	Race 3	*Ville de Paris* def *Challenge* (DNS)
	Race 4	*Il Moro* def *Tre Kronor* (DSQ)
Day 7	Race 1	*Tre Kronor* def *Challenge* (DNS)
	Race 2	*Ville de Paris* def *Il Moro* by 00:25
	Race 3	*New Zealand* def *Spirit* (DNS)
	Race 4	*Nippon* def *España 92* by 04:34

STANDINGS AFTER ROUND ROBIN 1:
New Zealand 6 points; *Il Moro* 5 points;
Nippon 6 points; *Ville de Paris* 5 points;
España 92 2 points; *Spirit* 3 points;
Tre Kronor 1 point; *Challenge* 0 points;

CHALLENGER ROUND ROBIN 2

February 15 - February 23, 1992
Total number of races: 28   Points per win: 4

Day 1	Race 1	*Nippon* def *Ville de Paris* by 01:42
	Race 2	*Il Moro* def *Tre Kronor* by 13:32
	Race 3	*España 92* def *Challenge* by 05:46
	Race 4	*New Zealand* def *Spirit* by 12:12
Day 2	Race 1	*New Zealand* def *España 92* by 04:55
	Race 2	*Spirit* def *Challenge* by 02:28
	Race 3	*Il Moro* def *Ville de Paris* by 00:11
	Race 4	*Nippon* def *Tre Kronor* by 02:21
Day 3	Race 1	*España 92* def *Tre Kronor* (DNF)
	Race 2	*New Zealand* def *Nippon* by 02:21

Race 3	*Ville de Paris* def *Spirit* by 01:48
Race 4	*Il Moro* def *Challenge* by 06:57
Day 4	Race 1	*New Zealand* def *Il Moro* by 01:16
	Race 2	*Spirit* def *Tre Kronor* by 02:52
	Race 3	*Nippon* def *Challenge* by 03:33
	Race 4	*Ville de Paris* def *España 92* by 03:07
Day 5	Race 1	*Il Moro* def *Spirit* by 07:58
	Race 2	*Nippon* def *España 92* by 04:12
	Race 3	*New Zealand* def *Tre Kronor* by 05:37
	Race 4	*Ville de Paris* def *Challenge* by 07:18
Day 6	Race 1	*Nippon* def *Spirit* by 12:21
	Race 2	*Il Moro* def *España 92* by 13:58
	Race 3	*Tre Kronor* def *Challenge* by 06:59
	Race 4	*New Zealand* def *Ville de Paris* by 00:08
Day 7	Race 1	*New Zealand* def *Challenge* by 06:46
	Race 2	*Ville de Paris* def *Tre Kronor* by 02:02
	Race 3	*Il Moro* def *Nippon* by 00:46
	Race 4	*España 92* def *Spirit* by 01:25

STANDINGS AFTER ROUND ROBIN 2:
New Zealand 34 points; *Il Moro* 29 points;
Nippon 26 points; *Ville de Paris* 21 points;
España 92 14 points; *Spirit* 11 points;
Tre Kronor 5 points; *Challenge* 0 points;

CHALLENGER ROUND ROBIN 3

March 8 - March 19, 1992
Total number of races: 28   Points per win: 8

Day 1	Race 1	*España 92* def *Tre Kronor* by 04:39
	Race 2	*Ville de Paris* def *New Zealand* by 01:21
	Race 3	*Nippon* def *Spirit* by 04:45
	Race 4	*Il Moro* def *Challenge* by 08:03
Day 2	Race 1	*Challenge* def *Spirit* by 02:45
	Race 2	*Nippon* def *Il Moro* by 00:05
	Race 3	*Ville de Paris* def *Tre Kronor* by 22:32
	Race 4	*New Zealand* def *España 92* by 17:46
Day 3	Race 1	*New Zealand* def *Spirit* by 08:10
	Race 2	*España 92* def *Challenge* (DNF)
	Race 3	*Il Moro* def *Tre Kronor* by 04:57
	Race 4	*Nippon* def *Ville de Paris* by 00:46
Day 4	Race 1	*Ville de Paris* def *Challenge* by 12:44
	Race 2	*New Zealand* def *Il Moro* by 05:01
	Race 3	*Nippon* def *España 92* by 04:13
	Race 4	*Spirit* def *Tre Kronor* by 06:42
Day 5	Race 1	*Il Moro* def *Ville de Paris* by 03:14
	Race 2	*Spirit* def *España 92* by 11:11
	Race 3	*New Zealand* def *Challenge* by 42:38
	Race 4	*Nippon* def *Tre Kronor* by 05:00
Day 6	Race 1	*Il Moro* def *España 92* by 02:14
	Race 2	*Ville de Paris* def *Spirit* by 03:13
	Race 3	*Nippon* def *New Zealand* by 01:02
	Race 4	*Tre Kronor* def *Challenge* by 01:13
Day 7	Race 1	*Nippon* def *Challenge* by 09:55

Race 2	*New Zealand* def *Tre Kronor* by 06:11
Race 3	*Ville de Paris* def *España 92* by 01:38
Race 4	*Il Moro* def *Spirit* by 01:15

STANDINGS AFTER ROUND ROBIN 3:
Nippon 82 points; *New Zealand* 74 points;
Il Moro 69 points; *Ville de Paris* 61 points;
España 92 30 points; *Spirit* 27 points;
Tre Kronor 13 points; *Challenge* 8 points

CHALLENGER SEMIFINALS

March 29 - April 9, 1992
Total number of races: 18   Points per win: 1

Day 1	Race 1	*New Zealand* def *Nippon* by 01:43
	Race 2	*Il Moro* def *Ville de Paris* by 01:24
Day 2	Race 1	*Ville de Paris* def *New Zealand* by 01:46
	Race 2	*Il Moro* def *Nippon* by 02:04
Day 3	Race 1	*New Zealand* def *Il Moro* by 00:18
	Race 2	*Ville de Paris* def *Nippon* by 03:30
Day 4	Race 1	*Nippon* def *Ville de Paris* by 02:00
	Race 2	*Il Moro* def *New Zealand* (DNF)
Day 5	Race 1	*Ville de Paris* def *Il Moro* by 01:56
	Race 2	*New Zealand* def *Nippon* by 02:49
Day 6	Race 1	*New Zealand* def *Ville de Paris* by 03:11
	Race 2	*Il Moro* def *Nippon* by 01:53
Day 7	Race 1	*Il Moro* def *Ville de Paris* by 01:28
	Race 2	*New Zealand* def *Nippon* by 00:31
Day 8	Race 1	*Nippon* def *Il Moro* by 01:53
	Race 2	*New Zealand* def *Ville de Paris* by 03:30
Day 9	Race 1	*New Zealand* def *Il Moro* by 02:20
	Race 2	*Nippon* def *Ville de Paris* by 00:24

STANDINGS AFTER CHALLENGER SEMIFINALS:
New Zealand 7 points; *Il Moro* 5 points
Nippon 3 points; *Ville de Paris* 3 points

CHALLENGER FINALS

April 18 - April 30, 1992
Best of 9 races

Day 1	Race 1	*New Zealand* def *Il Moro* by 01:32
Day 2	Race 2	*Il Moro* def *New Zealand* by 00:01
Day 3	Race 3	*New Zealand* def *Il Moro* by 00:34
Day 4	Race 4	*New Zealand* def *Il Moro* by 02:26
Day 5	Race 5	*New Zealand* def *Il Moro* by 02:38
Day 6	Race 6	*Il Moro* def *New Zealand* by 00:43
Day 7	Race 7	*Il Moro* def *New Zealand* by 00:53
Day 8	Race 8	*Il Moro* def *New Zealand* by 00:20
Day 9	Race 9	*Il Moro* def *New Zealand* by 01:33

Il Moro di Venezia wins the Louis Vuitton Cup

DEFENDERS OF THE FAITH
1992 Defender Trials

DEFENDER ROUND ROBIN 1

January 14 - January 25, 1992
Points per win: 1

Day 1	Race 1	*Defiant* def *Stars & Stripes* by 01:34
Day 2	Race 2	*Stars & Stripes* def *Jayhawk* by 04:10
Day 3	Race 3	*Defiant* def *Jayhawk* by 03:47
Day 4	Race 4	*Defiant* def *Stars & Stripes* by 02:36
Day 5	Race 5	*Stars & Stripes* def *Jayhawk* by 00:30
Day 6	Race 6	*Defiant* def *Jayhawk* by 00:20
Day 7	Race 7	*Defiant* def *Stars & Stripes* by 00:50
Day 8	Race 8	*Stars & Stripes* def *Jayhawk* by 06:08
Day 9	Race 9	*Defiant* def *Jayhawk* by 01:59

STANDINGS AFTER DEFENDER ROUND ROBIN 1:
  Defiant (America³ slot A) 6 points;
  Stars & Stripes 3 points
  Jayhawk (America³ slot B) 0 points

DEFENDER ROUND ROBIN 2

February 8 - February 18, 1992
Points per win: 2

Day 1	Race 1	*America³* def *Stars & Stripes* by 06:23
Day 2	Race 2	*Defiant* def *Stars & Stripes* by 04:16
Day 3	Race 3	*America³* def *Defiant* by 00:49
Day 4	Race 4	*America³* def *Stars & Stripes* by 06:00
Day 5	Race 5	*Stars & Stripes* def *Defiant* by 00:55
Day 6	Race 6	*Defiant* def *America³* by 01:05
Day 7	Race 7	*America³* def *Stars & Stripes* by 04:33
Day 8	Race 8	*Stars & Stripes* def *Defiant* by 00:47
Day 9	Race 9	*America³* def *Defiant* by 00:38

STANDINGS AFTER DEFENDER ROUND ROBIN 2:
  America³ (America³ slot A) 16 points
  Stars & Stripes 7 points
  Defiant (America³ slot B) 4 points

DEFENDER ROUND ROBIN 3

March 3 - March 15, 1992
Points per win: 4

Day 1	Race 1	*America³* def *Stars & Stripes* by 01:11
Day 2	Race 2	*Stars & Stripes* def *Defiant* by 02:15
Day 3	Race 3	*America³* def *Defiant* (DNF)
Day 4	Race 4	*America³* def *Stars & Stripes* by 05:33
Day 5	Race 5	*Defiant* def *Stars & Stripes* by 01:19
Day 6	Race 6	*America³* def *Defiant* by 00:31
Day 7	Race 7	*America³* def *Stars & Stripes* (DNF)
Day 8	Race 8	*Defiant* def *Stars & Stripes* by 00:23
Day 9	Race 9	*America³* def *Defiant* by 00:55

Day 10	Race 10	*Stars & Stripes* def *America³* by 01:05
Day 11	Race 11	*Stars & Stripes* def *Defiant* by 00:38
Day 12	Races 12/13	*America³* def *Defiant* by 00:34/00:23

STANDINGS AFTER DEFENDER ROUND ROBIN 3:
  America³ (America³ slot A) 48 points
  Stars & Stripes 19 points
  Defiant (America³ slot B) 12 points

DEFENDER ROUND ROBIN 4

March 28 - April 12, 1992
Kanza starts round with 2 points;
Stars & Stripes with 1 point; America³ with 0 points
Points per win: 1

Day 1	Race 1	*Stars & Stripes* def *Kanza* by 02:27
Day 2	Race 2	*Stars & Stripes* def *America³* by 00:45
Day 3	Race 3	*Kanza* def *America³* 01:13
Day 4	Race 4	*Kanza* def *Stars & Stripes* by 00:42
Day 5	Race 5	*Stars & Stripes* def *America³* by 01:56
Day 6	Race 6	*America³* def *Kanza* by 00:34
Day 7	Race 7	*Kanza* def *Stars & Stripes* by 00:57
Day 8	Race 8	*America³* def *Stars & Stripes* by 02:08
Day 9	Race 9	*America³* def *Kanza* by 09:59
Day 10	Race 10	*Stars & Stripes* def *Kanza* by 01:11
Day 11	Race 11	*America³* def *Stars & Stripes* by 00:44
Day 12	Race 12	*America³* def *Kanza* (DNF)
Day 13	Sailoff	*Stars & Stripes* def *Kanza* by 02:12

America³ and *Stars & Stripes* advance to Defender Finals

DEFENDER FINALS

April 18 - April 30, 1992
Best of 13 races

Day 1	Race 1	*America³* def *Stars & Stripes* by 02:09
Day 2	Race 2	*America³* def *Stars & Stripes* by 01:47
Day 3	Race 3	*America³* def *Stars & Stripes* by 04:20
Day 4	Race 4	*Stars & Stripes* def *America³* by 00:39
Day 5	Race 5	*America³* def *Stars & Stripes* by 03:31
Day 6	Race 6	*Stars & Stripes* def *America³* by 02:18
Day 7	Race 7	*Stars & Stripes* def *America³* by 01:28
Day 8	Race 8	*Stars & Stripes* def *America³* by 01:47
Day 9	Race 9	*America³* def *Stars & Stripes* by 01:08
Day 10	Race 10	*America³* def *Stars & Stripes* by 01:43
Day 11	Race 11	*America³* def *Stars & Stripes* by 05:08

STANDINGS AFTER DEFENDER FINALS:
  America³ 7 points; *Stars & Stripes* 4 points

  America³ wins the Defender Finals

ABBREVIATIONS:
DNS: Did not start
DSQ: Disqualified
DNF: Did not finish
Spirit: Spirit of Australia
Challenge: Challenge Australia
Il Moro: Il Moro di Venezia

Defenders & Challengers 1851-1992

Year	Boat	Nation		Boat	Nation
1851	America	USA	def	15 British Yachts	England
1870	Magic	USA	def	Cambria	England
1871	Columbia/Sappho	USA	def	Livonia	England
1876	Madeleine	USA	def	Countess of Dufferin	Canada
1881	Mischief	USA	def	Atalanta	Canada
1885	Puritan	USA	def	Genesta	England
1886	Mayflower	USA	def	Galatea	England
1887	Volunteer	USA	def	Thistle	Scotland
1893	Vigilant	USA	def	Valkyrie II	England
1895	Defender	USA	def	Valkyrie III	England
1899	Columbia	USA	def	Shamrock	England
1901	Columbia	USA	def	Shamrock II	England
1903	Reliance	USA	def	Shamrock III	England
1920	Resolute	USA	def	Shamrock IV	England
1930	Enterprise	USA	def	Shamrock V	England
1934	Rainbow	USA	def	Endeavour	England
1937	Ranger	USA	def	Endeavour II	England
1958	Columbia	USA	def	Sceptre	England
1962	Weatherly	USA	def	Gretel	Australia
1964	Constellation	USA	def	Sovereign	England
1967	Intrepid	USA	def	Dame Pattie	Australia
1970	Intrepid	USA	def	Gretel II	Australia
1974	Courageous	USA	def	Southern Cross	Australia
1977	Courageous	USA	def	Australia	Australia
1980	Freedom	USA	def	Australia	Australia
1983	Australia II	Australia	def	Liberty	USA
1987	Stars & Stripes	USA	def	Kookabura III	Australia
1988	Stars & Stripes	USA	def	New Zealand	New Zealand
1992	America³	USA	def	Il Moro di Venezia	Italy

Selected Bibliography

Cameron, Robert and Morgan, Neil, *Above San Diego*, Cameron and Company, San Francisco, 1990.

Carlin, Katherine Eitzen and Brandes, Ray, *Coronado: The Enchanted Island*, Coronado Historical Association 1987.

Dear, Ian *Enterprise to Endeavour*, Dodd, Mead & Company, New York, 1977.

Ian Dear *The America's Cup: An Informal History*, Dodd, Mead & Company New York 1980.

Fanta, J. Julius, *Winning the America's Cup*, Sea Lore Publishing Company New York 1969.

Hoyt, Edwin P., *The Defenders* A.S. Barnes and Co., Inc. Cranbury, New Jersey 1969.

Hoyt, Edwin P., *Commodore Vanderbilt*, Reilly & Lee Co., Chicago, 1962.

Illingworth, Captain John H., *Twenty Challenges for the America's Cup*, St. Martin's Press New York 1968.

Levitt, Michael and Lloyd, Barbara, *Upset: Australia Wins the America's Cup*, Workman, New York, 1983.

LaDow, Charles R., *The Ships, the House, and the Men (A History of the San Diego Yacht Club)*, Frazee Industries, San Diego, 1977.

Lipton, Sir Thomas, *Lipton's Autobiography*, Duffield and Green, New York, 1932.

McGrew, Clarence Alan, *City of San Diego and San Diego County*, The American Historical Society, Chicago and New York, 1922.

Pourade, Richard, *The Explorers*, Union-Tribune Publishing Company, San Diego, 1960.

Richardson, Joanna, *Victoria & Albert*, Quadrangle/The New York Times Book Co., 1977.

Riegert, Ray, *California: The Ultimate Guidebook*, Ulysses Press, Berkeley, CA, 1990.

Riggs, Doug, *Keelhauled*, Seven Seas Press Inc., Newport, RI, 1986.

Rousmaniere, John, *The Low Black Schooner*, Mystic Seaport Museum Stores, Mystic, Connecticut, 1986.

Simon, Carey and Solomon, Charlene Marmer, *Frommer's California Kids*, Simon & Schuster, Inc. New York 1989.

Star, Raymond, *San Diego: A Pictorial History*, Donning Company/Publishers Norfolk, Virginia, 1986.

Sullaway, Neva, *Sailing in San Diego: A Pictorial History*, TCS Publishing , Inc. San Diego, 1991.

Tasker, Rolly, America's Cup collection.

Thompson, Winfield M. *The Lawson's History of the America's Cup*.

Periodicals

Chance, Britton, "Design," *Seahorse*, London, February 1992.

Lennox, Angus, "Lipton" *Nautical Quarterly*, New York, Issue 1, 1977.

Los Angeles *Times* — specifically the daily Cup coverage by Rich Roberts.

Rousmaniere, John "Keeping the Cup — 1870-1983" *Nautical Quarterly*, New York, Winter 1986.

Rousmaniere, John "The Bottom Line — Selecting the America's Cup Defender," *Nautical Quarterly* 11, 1980.

San Diego *Union/Tribune* — specifically the daily Cup coverage by Bill Center.

CHAPTER ONE PICTURE CREDITS

ACKNOWLEDGMENTS

The author is indebted to Mystic Seaport Museum, Mystic, Connecticut, for its permission to publish historical photographs from its Rosenfeld Collection and for its display at the America's Cup Museum in San Diego, a San Diego Unified Port District project. Also helpful was the Mystic Seaport Museum book, *The Low Black Schooner: Yacht America,* written by John Rousmaniere. The author also acknowledges the help of Michelle Button for compiling the race results. Drawings by Guy-Roland Perrin and Jacques Taglang were used as source material for Chris Lloyd's keel drawings in Chapter Two.